The Poetry of

William Carlos Williams

of Rutherford

Other Books of Essays
by Wendell Berry

The Poetry of

William Carlos Williams

of Rutherford

Wendell Berry

COUNTERPOINT

BERKELEY

Library of Congress Cataloging-in-Publication Data
Berry, Wendell, 1934–
The poetry of William Carlos Williams of Rutherford /
Wendell Berry.
p. cm.
ISBN-13: 978-1-58243-714-9
ISBN-10: 1-58243-714-9
1. Williams, William Carlos, 1883–1963—Criticism and
interpretation. 2. Williams, William Carlos, 1883–1963—
Influence. I. Title.
PS3545.I544Z575 2011
811'.52—dc22
2010030912

Jacket design by Ann Weinstock
Interior design by David Bullen
Printed in the United States of America

COUNTERPOINT
1919 Fifth Street
Berkeley, CA 94710

www.counterpointpress.com

Distributed by Publishers Group West

10 9 8 7 6 5 4 3 2 1

for Robert Hass

৪৫

The primitive destiny of the land is obscure, but it has been obscured further by a field of unrelated culture stuccoed upon it that has made that destiny more difficult than ever to determine. To this latter nearly all the aesthetic adhesions of the present day occur. Through that stratum of obscurity the acute but frail genius of the place must penetrate.

৪৫

All have to come from under and through a dead layer.

৪৫

He wants to have the feet of his understanding on the ground, his ground, the ground, the only ground that he knows, that which is under his feet.

William Carlos Williams, "Descent,"
from *In the American Grain*

Contents

The Poetry of

William Carlos Williams

of Rutherford

1

A Prologue

. . . .

    To the extent that a life can have an agenda, my life's agenda for a long time has included some sort of deliberative writing about the poetry of William Carlos Williams, not as an "objective" academic endeavor, for which I had no need, but rather as a payment or at least an acknowledgement of a personal debt. I would need to do this late in my life, I thought, the better to understand both Williams' effort and my own, and therefore the character and size of my debt to him. Through most of my life as a writer, I have taken an increasingly familiar pleasure and an invaluable sustenance and reassurance from his poetry. And there was a time in my early years, as I was struggling to find my way through much misapprehension and error, when his example was indispensable.

    As a young man trying to become a writer, I had undoubtedly a few advantages. From my mother, who reportedly read to me from the romantic poets virtually from the time of my birth, I had the love of reading. From my father, a farmer and lawyer, an advocate all his life for the small farmers of our region, and who never spoke except with care, I received a conscientious and sometimes urgent sense of the movement and syntax of sentences. Both of my parents were attentive to the correctness of diction, pronunciation, and grammar, which of course in my youthful rebelliousness I ignored, and by which of course I was powerfully influenced.

Moreover, I grew up within a few miles of both sets of my grandparents and many other relatives in the place where, with the exception of one great-grandfather, my family had lived during all of its known history, beginning early in the pioneer times of Kentucky. I had heard, as a child in the womb and from then on, the speech indigenous to the place. My best gift as a writer, as I was late in realizing, was this local language uninfluenced throughout my formative years by the electronic media. In those years I was also influenced by regular exposure to the language of the King James Bible and of hymns, to the language of books that were read to me and that I later read for myself, and to a sizable repertory of obscene poems and songs that were sometimes fairly scrupulously metered and rhymed.

When I entered the University of Kentucky in the fall of 1952, wishing by then to learn to be a writer, I was fairly literate and wrote well enough to make good grades on essays assigned by my teachers and to answer competently the "essay questions" on examinations, at least when I had bothered to study enough.

But acquiring for myself an art of poetry, insofar as I may have done so, was far more difficult than writing pretty good student papers. I have never learned anything easily. The memory of my early efforts to write poems that would satisfy my developing sense of what a poem might be is dreadful to me now. I tried to write like T. S. Eliot, Robert Frost, Dylan Thomas, and others. These were not lengthy efforts. However long the desire might last, the failures happened quickly and were definitive. I hadn't read or worked or lived long enough to *absorb* an influence to any constructive purpose, and I lacked the facility for credible imitation. I made only messes, recognized them as such, suffered the failures, and tried something else.

One of my problems was too general an ambition. Without any consideration specifically of myself and of my own needs, abilities, and limitations, I simply wanted to be a poet, to write poems that would be admired and published. I would have been equally pleased to have been the author of poems like Eliot's or Frost's or Thomas's—or, for that matter, poems like those of Keats or Marvell or Herrick.

Another problem was the vogue among my teachers and friends, the magazines and the critics, of the doctrine of originality. Somewhere vaguely beyond my idea of writing "like" some poet I admired, was the idea that I might write something "original," something as unforeseen and world-shaking, maybe, as *The Waste Land*.

All this was hopeless because I had so little and so poorly understood myself. I had allowed and even taught myself to aspire to the life of a writer entirely without respect to the life I had been born to and so far, except for school, had lived. With the help of my schooling, my teachers, my contemporaries and friends, and much of my reading, I was thinking of myself as a young man of the modern age who would inhabit a career rather than a place. In the process I was ignoring or depreciating everything that had made me the young man I actually was, including chiefly the small countryside and neighborhood that I had known from birth.

My friend Robert B. Weeden, the biologist and writer, recently sent me several pages on which he had gathered a selection of interesting items, among them the following: "Infant humans have special areas in the cortex where they remember human faces (but not names), and another area where they build memory maps of landscapes." I am strongly prejudiced against the anatomizing of things I have perceived and respected as whole, but this particular sentence I have clung to as something needed. It suggests and seems to respect the possibility that my mind, as I am a placed person, may have been formed from birth by memories, an active knowledge, of the faces and the countryside that surrounded me, drawing my interest and my love, during all my young life.

I was, in truth, an anachronism, a young old-timer, and though I had little conscious or workable self-knowledge, I was divided and troubled in my mind. On the one hand, I was doing my best to welcome and participate in the industrialization and modernization of society following World War II. On the other hand, I kept a profound allegiance to my small "provincial" home country, and just as profound an affection for its old life both as I had learned it from my elders and as I had lived it before, during, and in the years immediately following the war.

Though I would espouse noisily certain progressive or forward-looking ideas—including, to my embarrassment now, school consolidation—I was nonetheless a kind of conservative, not in the presently corrupt and meaningless sense of that term, but in the sense of wishing to conserve or of reluctantly giving up certain "old-fashioned" things that I loved and perceived as worthy. I was reflexively opposed to any technological developments that destroyed land, and to the use of eminent domain for such purposes. I was unpersuaded by the justifying rhetorics. Because from childhood I had participated in the necessarily physical work of what I can only call the real world, I seem to have been constitutionally debarred from the least belief in the technological paradise that was being hawked about by ad-writers, boosters, and politicians. I could not accept the required "trade-off" of neighborliness for monstrosity.

As a matter of fact, I had first thought of becoming a writer because of my belief that my native place and neighborhood had given me knowledge worthy of writing. And so I was wrong—misled and self-deceiving—in my efforts to become in some general or professional or "original" way a poet. This was an instance, as Robert Duncan put it, of "originality that tries to hold out against origins."[1] I was a long time discovering that I needed to learn to write authentically what I authentically knew.

This was going to require a certain defiance. By 1961 I had gained enough confidence to show a proposed book of poems to a reputable editor, who passed the typescript to a "reader" (a young poet, as I understood), who handed down the single judgment that I was employing the wrong "subject matter." The real, the only real, subject of poetry in the modern age, so the reader said, was "the city." Since then, I know, my work has sometimes again met this obstruction, and may have met it more often than I know: the apparent disbelief in the importance of anything or any issue outside the limits of the major cities, as if the very food people eat generates spontaneously on the shelves of grocery stores.

ᚼᚭ

William Carlos Williams was not one of the poets I most cherished in my student days or tried to imitate. I did not read him at length or carefully until the summer of 1957, after my formal education ended. I owned by then the two volumes of *The Collected Earlier Poems* and *The Collected Later Poems* and a copy of *Journey to Love*. I read these books, as it happened, not at school, but in one of the dearest places of my home country, an old family "camp house" beside the Kentucky River. By that time I had gotten beyond the frustrating urge to imitate the work of any poet who appealed to me, and so was capable of being actually influenced by it.

Also, as I read and wrote through that summer and took part, as I always had, in the work of farms I had always known, I was beginning the long growth and effort of recognizing my place, and myself as a part of it, belonging to it. Williams, though I was not adequately conscious of it then, had made a similar "journey," his beginnings as a poet probably as awkward as my own. Of his early poem, "First Praise," he said, "I should have written about things around me, but I didn't know how."[2]

I am not undertaking here a defense or justification of my own poetry, which of course cannot be my business. My concern, rather, is with local adaptation, an issue of history, culture, and geography to which poetry is subordinate though necessary. Local adaptation, as a personal obligation and effort, is as far as possible from the famous "identity crisis." It has nothing to do with self-discovery as a single or autonomous individual. It has everything to do with discovering where one is in relation to one's place (native or chosen), to its natural and human neighborhood, to its mystery and sanctity, and with discovering right ways of living and working there.

To put Williams' work under the heading of local adaptation seems to me appropriate, as I am going to try to show. And from his example I learned to put my own work under that heading, to see it not as an end in itself but as a part of a necessary, if never finished or finishable, effort to belong authentically where my life had put me.

Though I was born and bred a countryman and Williams was natively urban (and far more understandingly urban than I was rural), as I read his poems that summer in a place so congenial to my mind, they seemed oddly to fit. They fit not so much the place as my imagination and my need in that place. By the record of his long attending to his place, and his long search for a right way to speak of it, I was learning, somewhat

A Prologue

deliberately at last, to pay attention to my own place. To me at that time, as I can now see, his work was a gift immeasurably useful and valuable.

I would be wrong to leave the impression that I then knew competently or very consciously what was going on with me. I was twenty-three in the summer of 1957. I still assumed, as my schooling had taught me, and as I would continue to assume for the next seven years, that I would not live at home, but would make my way, who knew where, as some sort of literary careerist. I had turned almost entirely by necessity to my home place for "subject matter," for in fact I had no other place to turn, and by an intuition related to that necessity I was becoming a sort of follower or student—though I think not much an imitator—of Williams.

My interest in his work of course got around among my friends and their friends, and so my reading of his poems began to be accompanied by voices, some that I had to hear with respect, telling me pointedly that Williams was not the right influence for a young poet. The criticisms of him and his work generally reduced to the charge of "mindlessness," in the sense both of unintelligent and of artistic regardlessness. Williams seemed often to have been personally endearing to people who did not like his work. And so I would hear, sometimes from older writers I admired, judgments such as "I love Bill Williams, but he has no mind."

That judgment on the part of some critics survived Williams by at least a quarter of a century. By then my subject had become again and finally my home, I was fully settled also in

my respect for Williams and his work, and I knew better than
to give that accusation of "mindlessness" the time of day. But
I had had to contend with it, and late into the drafting of this
book I still felt the need to begin by defending him. Finally,
however, I saw that defense was not necessary. If some of his
critics had been dismissive of his work, that dismissal was sufficiently answered for my own purposes by my own long respect
for his work and my understanding of its usefulness.

If, as I am told, Williams is now generally admired in the
English departments, that likewise is of no interest to me here.
My purpose in this writing is to say as exactly as I can what I
see as useful in his poetry. To me, it has been useful and sustaining as evidence, even as a history, of Williams' lifelong effort to
come to terms with, to imagine, and to be of use to his native
and chosen place. This is the effort of what is properly called
"local adaptation," of increasing concern to him and similarly
to me, but a subject virtually of no interest, so far as I know, in
any departments of the modern university. The effort to adapt
the economic life of a human community to the nature of its
place is an effort intricately cultural, involving the relation of
all work, including poetry, to "the ground underfoot," and
involving inevitably the quality of that relation. And so my
concern is equally with the usefulness and the quality of Williams' poetry.

The Struggle Toward a Credible Language

. . . .

The truths of settled convention, like the truths of empirical science, are static, predictable, nailed down, whereas Williams dedicated his poetry to confrontation with the flux and diversity of the world and of our experience of it. The world, as he saw it from the vantage of Rutherford or Paterson, New Jersey, was always breaking out of the settled categories, sortings, and abstractions of minds that are academic or encyclopedic:

A flower within a flower whose history
(within the mind) crouching

among the ferny rocks, laughs at the names
by which they think to trap it. Escapes!

. . . .

The vague accuracies of events dancing two
and two with language which they
forever surpass . . . [1]

These shape-shiftings present themselves by way of art, not
to any established coherence of science or understanding, but
to the senses, to affection, and finally—so Williams hoped and
so must we all—to imagination. I will come back to this issue of
art and imagination. I mention it now only to suggest that the
relation of art and coherence, as Williams saw it, is not simple
and is never finally settled. In his effort to understand himself
and do his work as an American poet, he had before him the
example of Whitman and Whitman's passion to include everything. But Williams also put before himself the inevitability that
artists, and especially local artists, living at home, returning to
the same places and people day after day, year after year, will
be faced with circumstances and experiences that their art, as
they have received or so far made it, cannot include.

I think that Williams addressed these questions consciously
and directly. And though apparently never satisfied with the
results, he made a respectable and useful attempt to answer.
But first let us look at an example of what, at his best, he made
himself capable of writing:

The Poetry of William Carlos Williams of Rutherford

A Negro Woman

carrying a bunch of marigolds
      wrapped
            in an old newspaper:
She carries them upright,
      bareheaded,
            the bulk
of her thighs
      causing her to waddle
            as she walks
looking into
      the store window which she passes
            on her way.
What is she
      but an ambassador
            from another world
a world of pretty marigolds
      of two shades
            which she announces
not knowing what she does
      other
            than walk the streets
holding the flowers upright
      as a torch
            so early in the morning.[2]

The Struggle Toward a Credible Language

This is the first poem of *Journey to Love*, published in 1955. Since I first read it in 1957, I have read this poem many times. For me, it has retained the "irrepressible freshness" that Pound attributed to "classic" poetry.[3] Because of this indomitable freshness, "for ever new," I have never read it inattentively or without love for it. We may conclude from his "anti-poetic" subject,[4] as no doubt many have concluded, that Williams lacked the visionary power of Blake or Yeats. But we had better be careful. As this poem shows, Williams had the power to see the unique, ordinary lives of his place in, so to speak, their glory.

The image of a woman carrying "a bunch" of autumn flowers had been on Williams' mind for a long time. She appears around 1940 in "A Portrait of the Times," a poem that seems merely realistic in its dispassion, and careless in the grammatical uncertainty of "them." At first we are shown "two W.P.A. men," and then:

> . . . an old
> squint-eyed woman
> in a black
>
> dress
> and clutching
> a bunch of

late chrysanthemums
to her
fatted bosoms

turned her back
on them
at the corner [5]

Going from this to "A Negro Woman," we see how appreci-
ably this figure had gathered light to itself over the intervening
years. In the later poem the poet's eye for "realistic" detail is
still acute, but this poem reaches far higher than realism. The
difference is partly made by a simile (the flowers are carried "as
a torch"), partly by an enlargement of imagination, and partly
by a commensurate increase of lyricism and luminosity. The
woman brings light "from another world" to light this world,
and she in turn is lighted by imagination. Only imagination,
which is aware of "the mystery / of these streets" and the "holiness" of ordinary things,[6] which "knows all stories / before they
are told,"[7] could so illuminate a "realistic" scene. The "other
world" from which she comes is the world of imagination in
which she is timelessly real; she is an "ambassador" because
she has come to assure us of this. The poem has a quality of
myth—we may remember Persephone or even Prometheus—
but though it conforms exactly to no myth that I know, it shim-
mers and resounds in the way of the oldest stories.

As for the poem's lyricism, the chiming particularly of the

The Struggle Toward a Credible Language

assonances will be audible to any attentive reader. But what I want most to call attention to is the poem's rhythmic integrity. To use the word that Williams himself used repeatedly and that named his chief technical concern, the poem is astutely and assuredly *measured*. To see that it is, you probably should not try to sound it as a composition of "variable feet"—Williams' prosodic invention that has never made sense to me. Instead, read it aloud according to a natural and regular rhythm, without insisting that there should be a sound for every beat, inflecting according to the line breaks, the punctuation, and the sense of the sentences and the syntax. You will speak the poem then as a sort of chant, modulating on the strong assonance of "so" into the folk refrain, "so early in the morning."

This poem seems to me as nearly perfect as any I know. What does it "mean"? There is no explanatory construct of thought that anybody can stand beside this poem to help "understand" it. That it cannot be explained is intrinsic to its character and quality. After you have read it, you know something beautiful and consoling that you did not know before. It means what it says. Thoreau wished to speak as "a man in his waking moments." When Williams wrote this poem, and many others, he was a man extraordinarily awake.

❧

If Williams in his last years was capable of writing a poem so nearly perfect, both imaginatively and technically, it seems merely cautious to suppose that this was not accidental and that "A Negro Woman" is not anomalous. It is true that Williams did not mature early as a poet. Some of the early work is simply bad, though there are a few satisfactory poems among the earliest. But signs of struggle are everywhere, and the struggle appears to have been purposeful. He was working according to a felt standard or intuition of verse-making, hard to articulate, but which nevertheless lured him on to try again and again, and which in the long run served him well. He was trying to find a credible language with which to speak of the life around him. And his work was improving. The second version of "Pastoral I" is remarkably better than the first. By 1916 when he was thirty-three, he wrote this, which ought to have notified the skeptics that something remarkable was under way:

> It's a strange courage
> you give me ancient star:
>
> Shine alone in the sunrise
> toward which you lend no part![8]

He wrote a number of worthy poems before he published *Sour Grapes* in 1921, the year he was thirty-eight. By then, though the struggle visibly continued as it was to do until the end of his life, he was writing with assurance and an always clearer sense of the work he was trying to do. By 1934 when he was fifty-

The Struggle Toward a Credible Language

one, to give an example that by its brevity and modesty may display his technical competence and confidence more clearly than something more ambitious, he wrote this:

> She sits with
> tears on
>
> her cheek
> her cheek on
>
> her hand
> the child
>
> in her lap
> his nose
>
> pressed
> to the glass [9]

He was learning to make of his own language a work that could be nothing but a poem — that could not be replaced by a picture, say, or by anything in prose.

The Kind
of Poet
He Was

. . . .

It is necessary, in fairness and in simple courtesy, to ask what kind of poet Williams was. The answer clearly begins with his failure to conform to the usual expectations.

The now-prevailing idea seems to be that poets occupy their designated place in the departmented structure of the arts and sciences, of which the increasingly industrialized modern university is the model. Poets, that is to say, are professionals like other professionals and specialists like other specialists. Their business is to produce, ideally, perfect poems of lasting value individually, as objects of art or "high culture." This assumption seems to underlie the judgment of such dismissive critics as Donald Davie and Bruce Bawer. Precedent to them was Yvor Winters, who, admirable as he was in some ways, ranked individual poems as greatest ever, greatest in English, etc., as if the art of poetry were a sort of contest. Increasingly, moreover, poets are attached to universities and are dependent upon them for a living. I have been at times so attached and so dependent myself, and thus I know something of what is involved. Unless university poets are actually from some place in particular, and unless they have the good fortune to be employed somewhere near their homes, they tend to be careerists and migrants, without local knowledge or affection or loyalty, like their professional and specialist colleagues. They are therefore under pressure to conform to, and they have no immediate reason to resist, the industrialist order represented by their university. They, like their critics, are inclined to think that the arts are under obligation to keep up with the times, and to conform to industrial values and the advances of technology. This is not a quarrel I wish to bring against anybody in particular, and I know there are reasons and also exceptions. (The most admirable exceptions are the ones who, despite the pressure to "produce" research and publications, have been steadily devoted to their teaching, their subjects, and their students.) What I am describing, however, is too easily possible in modern universities. The tendency is toward careerism, personal displacement, scientific reductionism, and technological determinism. Williams saw this tendency, understood it, feared it, and resisted it.

He himself was not the least bit academic, either in his life or in his language. (Donald Davie took him to task for never using the word "enjambment.") He lived, practiced medicine, and wrote his poems in the same place all his life. He lived by the terms of a community involvement more constant, more intimate, and more urgent than that of any other notable poet of his time. He watched his neighbors and his patients, who often were the same people, with the keenest interest, affection, and amusement, and often enough with dismay. That he greatly loved at least some of those he served we have testimony both in his poetry and in such lovely stories as "Ancient Gentility" and "A Night in June." Though he was trained as a pediatrician, by the evidence of his writings his practice was not specialized. The doctor in "Ancient Gentility" cares for an elderly woman. "A Night in June" is the story of a baby's birth. He wrote his poetry in the course of his daily confrontation, as a doctor and a neighbor, with "the pure products of America [going] crazy."[1] It was this craziness, well understood and properly feared, that kept him from resting satisfied even with his best poems. He kept trying to extend the reach and comprehensiveness of his art, and so to make a language "to reconcile / the people and the stones," as he put it in one of his exemplary short poems.[2] A doctor who ministers to his home community and his neighbors is not in the modern sense a specialist, because he is also, always and at the same time, a neighbor and a citizen. A poet who is a doctor who is a community member likewise is not, because he cannot be, in the modern sense a specialist.

That defines, perhaps fully enough, the kind of poet Williams was. He was a poet determinedly and conscientiously local. Some writers, comparatively few, have assumed the burden both of local subject matter and local stewardship, and some—most—do not. Thoreau did, Henry James did not;

Faulkner did, Hemingway did not; Williams did, Eliot did not. By noticing this, I mean to imply no blame. The difference is nonetheless significant, and it must be taken into account if we are to deal justly with Williams' poetry. As Booker T. Washington counseled his own people to do, Williams cast down his bucket where he was.

The Problems of a Local Commitment

. . . .

The locally committed poet in America assumes a predicament and a difficulty that requires some care to define. To commit oneself to write in and about an American place that is not New York City and is therefore a "provincial" place—especially perhaps for writers of Williams' generation—was to be faced with a subject that was in a sense culturally unprecedented. It was, as Williams wrote in the first book of *Paterson*, "to confront a mass of detail / to interrelate on a new ground, difficultly / . . . pulling the disparate together to clarify / and compress . . ."[1]

The problem, rightly named, is that of "a new ground." America was, to Europe and to the deracinated Europeans who claimed it, a new place, unprotected by the cultural restraints of the Old World and therefore vulnerable to the Old World's worst impulses and desires. America was "discovered" as one of the results of the broken coherence, such as it was, of medieval Europe. Its discoverers and claimants, from Columbus to the corporate free-marketers of our day, have been predominantly of the sort that Wallace Stegner called "boomers" — people who have come only to take and sell whatever they could tear loose, giving nothing in return. The evidence of this, of course, is the belatedly recognized "crisis" of the uninhabitable abstraction miscalled "the environment." Culturally, until Williams' time and increasingly from then until now, most Americans have been exiles and strangers. And so, near the end of his life, Williams could speak of Columbus's voyage

> which promised so much
>> but due to the world's avarice
>>> breeding hatred
> through fear
>> ended so disastrously . . .[2]

and cry out that "Waste, waste! / dominates the world." [3]

In this condition of general displacement and estrangement, regardlessness and waste, Williams determined to live, as a doctor and a poet, in his native place where he started his medical practice in 1910. In the following half century he would work and think and write his way into the implications of this choice. The first, and the most formidable and lasting, of these implications that he dealt with as a poet was the mass of local details, never until then adequately accommodated in his language, that came crowding into his mind: details of geography, of daily work, of local life and economy, and of course the details of an imposed industrialism and its overwhelming power to uproot, alienate, and corrupt.

To take this on was a task of enormous difficulty. Williams seems to have spent a long time and a lot of effort just in recognizing the extent of the difficulty. He must have been virtually alone in knowing that such a task existed or was possible, and few know it even now. Expatriation was the literary norm or ideal of Williams' contemporaries. Williams spent a year of his boyhood in a Swiss school, but though he traveled in Europe extensively as an adult, he never again lived there. This apparently makes it possible to think of him as a defective member of his literary generation. According to Bruce Bawer, "Williams did not join the exodus to Europe . . . because he didn't have the nerve to leave home."[4] This possibility, though almost certainly untrue, seems to have worried Williams himself. To be a solitary exception to the rule, to be largely absent from the defining experience of his literary generation, surely cost him some discomfort and some doubt. An ironic notice of his predicament was that *The Descent of Winter*, a sequence of poems begun as he returned from a visit to Europe and continued as he took up again his task of making poems of the local sights, sounds, and voices of Rutherford, was first published in *The Exile*, edited by Ezra Pound.

The Problems of a Local Commitment

There is in *Paterson*, Book Two, a passage addressed to a "you" of obscure reference, in which Williams is explicitly arguing his case for staying in Rutherford despite difficulties that led him, sometimes at least, to despair. The "you" of the passage seems to be the place, which would be, wherever he might go, his subject:

> Why should I move from this place
> where I was born? knowing
> how futile would be the search
> for you in the multiplicity
> of your debacle. The world spreads
> for me like a flower opening—and
> will close for me as might a rose—
>
> wither and fall to the ground
> and rot and be drawn up
> into a flower again. But you
> never wither—but blossom
> all about me. In that I forget
> myself perpetually—in your
> composition and decomposition
> I find my   .   .
>   despair!⁵

Staying and accomplishing his work at home required extraordinary courage and persistence. Living in Europe, for those who did so, was a cutting loose from home. By that the expatriates were freed of the mass of detail that weighed upon Williams in Rutherford. In his favor he had his inborn relish and affection for these details. But what was he to do with them? He needed to gather them in and somehow make order and sense of them. For this the traditional formality seemed to him too exclusive and imbued with cultural attitudes and expectations that belonged properly elsewhere.

Whitman's work, one might think, would have offered Williams a useful precedent. Whitman had dealt with the "new ground" problem and American experience by gathering up details out of the mass into the centripetal rhetoric of his long lines, which to my ear work authentically as lines, as poetry, but which have the weakness of all-inclusiveness, and often the weakness also of affirming or approving everything they are able to include. Williams needed an art more precisely forceful and more discriminating.

His commitment to one small part of the world made him radical in a way that he may only partly have recognized—that undoubtedly is more recognizable now than it was, even to him, during his lifetime. The issue he raised by deciding to live and work at home in a "province" of New Jersey, an issue that by now is becoming prominent and urgent, was that of context, of local adaptation. By staying put, Williams was forcing himself to learn, however stumblingly or "difficultly" at first, that the condition of the place, its *health* in the fullest sense, was necessarily one of the measures of the quality of the work that was done in it. Poetry, which for other poets was personal or "cultural," became for Williams a civic obligation, a kind of work relating to community membership and neighborhood.

And so his poetry sometimes has a spokesmanly didacticism, from as early as "Tract" of 1916—"I will teach you my towns-people / how to perform a funeral . . ."[6]—to "The Problem" of 1953:

> How to fit
>> an old brownstone church
>>> among a group
> of modern office buildings:
>> The feat stands,
>>> so that the argument
> must be after the fact.
>> We can learn from it
>>> how—
> if it is not too late—
>> to conduct
>>> our lives.
> . . . .
>
>>> Witness merely how
> in the morning light
>> it preserves itself,
>>> how confidently,
> and without strain,
>> it faces the world.

                              As if,

        and indeed it is so,

                    should it be tumbled down,

                              nothing

        could replace it.7

Sometimes the imperative is tacit: Look. Listen. Taste. Smell.
Feel. Think. Pay attention. Know these lives, these things, these
stories with which you share this place. Sometimes, as in the
examples above, it is explicit and forthright. The poet is speaking in his poems of a shared place; he is speaking first of all to his
fellow sharers. The poems therefore needed to be written in a
shared language, a tongue common to the poet and his readers,
even to his neighbors who may never read him. This is the
reason for Williams' preoccupation with what he called "the
American idiom," a subject to which I will need to return.

Local
Adaptation

. . . .

Williams in his writing moved more and more decisively toward a sense of the poet as a local maker of a kind of order, a spokesman and teacher. Another name for his task is "local adaptation." Since his time, the understanding of place as the right context and measure of work has become as urgent and articulate among some scientists as among some poets. It began, I am supposing, with Aldo Leopold's restorative work and thought on his plowed-to-exhaustion Sand County farm. But perhaps it would have been hard for any ecologist seriously devoted to a place to miss the point.

In my own reading, the Canadian ecologist Stan Rowe is the most thorough and clarifying, on this issue of place, especially in his insistence that the next order above or beyond organisms is the ecosystem—*not* the "environment" or the "biosphere." Ecology, he wrote, "invites the study of the world's living spaces and all that is within them."[1] By "all" he meant both the living creatures, the organisms, and the nonliving: the water, the light, the stones. He wrote further that "Ecology is the science of context . . . [which] teaches the absolute dependence of things [including, of course, the humans] on what is peripheral to them . . . "[2]

More specifically to my purpose here, Rowe denied absolutely "the theory that we are fundamentally creatures of culture," to whom "virtual reality" is as good as reality. His point, which here converges with one of Williams' concerns, is that cultures can be wrong: "Culture, carried and transmitted by language, can also conceal fundamentals." Cultures can be ecologically unsustainable. And wrong cultures can cause people to "feel like strangers on Earth, fearful and alienated."[3]

The thinking of Stan Rowe, in turn, has directly informed and encouraged the work of Wes Jackson and his colleagues at The Land Institute in Salina, Kansas. The major project of The Land Institute scientists is not to "revolutionize" agriculture technologically (and disastrously) as has been the way of the industrialists, but rather to re-form it in harmony with its local context of ecological processes and limits—hence their effort to replace ecologically weak and damaging monocultures of annual crops with ecologically strong and conserving polycultures of perennials. Since this work is taking place in Kansas, these scientists have accepted absolutely the context of the local tallgrass prairie ecosystem as both the model and the measure of their work. This science is unofficial, noncommercial, selflessly motivated, locally focused and adapted, and measured always by the complex standard of ecological and community health. It is only within accepted limits that the possibilities of coherence, form, and durability begin to emerge. These possibilities are not inherent in thoughts or projects that are limitless in scale or universal in application.

If we think now of the conviviality between the work of an ecologically literate, locally committed poet such as Gary Snyder and this kind of science in agriculture and forestry, we become aware of an incipient and necessary cultural change that authenticates Williams' example in a way he could not have anticipated. We are seeing the emergence of stewardly arts and sciences, submitted to the service and good-keeping of home places, as opposed to the triumphal arts and sciences of individual genius and ambition that still are dominant in the universities, where the specialist or professional career, not a place, is the context of work.

သင်

But to say that Williams' work has lived into a time when it is more pertinent and more needed than before is not to say that he was in his own time an anomaly. He was then unenviable, not to say unfashionable, in his choice of place, and he knew it. But there had been, and there were, others like him, and he also knew that.

I don't think Williams could have seen exactly eye-to-eye with Thoreau. Rutherford was no more Concord than it was New York. But they were temperamentally different also, and Thoreau's language, good as it was, would not have suited Williams. To Williams, and he was hardly alone, it must have seemed that American literature waited a long time for the coming of Huckleberry Finn, and Thoreau had been dead twenty-three years before the arrival of Huck. But Thoreau lived, wrote, and made what passed with him for a living, in his native community, which he knew intimately and wrote about in detail. When Thoreau said he had traveled much in Concord, Williams, who had traveled much in Rutherford, would have known what he meant.

Among Williams' acknowledged heroes was the French entomologist Jean-Henri Fabre (1823–1915). Williams must have enjoyed Fabre's spur-of-the-moment science, sufficiently akin to that of a family doctor, but no doubt he was also encouraged and consoled by Fabre's long and devoted attention to the insect and other life of his tiny *harmas* in southern France. It is not hard to imagine the delight and the sense of companionship and confirmation with which Williams might have read the following sentences addressed by Fabre to his friends the insects:

> Others again have reproached me with my style, which has not the solemnity, nay, better, the dryness of the schools. They fear lest a page that is read without fatigue should not always be the expression of the truth. Were I to take their word for it, we are profound only on condition of being obscure. Come here, one and all of you—you, the sting-bearers, and you, the wing-cased armour-clads—

take up my defense and bear witness in my favor. Tell of the intimate terms on which I live with you, of the patience with which I observe you, of the care with which I record your actions.

—or, isolated in his province as he was, how Williams would have relished this:

Eden, I said; and, from the point of view that interests me, the expression is not out of place. This cursed ground, which no one would have had at a gift to sow with a pinch of turnip-seed, is an earthly paradise for the Bees and Wasps.[4]

Another of Williams' heroes, another Frenchman whose life overlapped with his own, was Paul Cézanne. When he referred to Cézanne, Williams was likely to be thinking about technique. Cézanne, like Juan Gris and others, did not merely copy or "plagiarize" nature, but rather made a work of art newly imagined. And yet it would have mattered necessarily to Williams that Cézanne returned again and again to the *motif* of his native countryside.

But after thinking of both of them for many years, I believe that the person to whom Williams can be most suggestively compared is his younger contemporary, William Faulkner. They are nothing alike in their ways of writing or in their subjects. They dealt with two distinct varieties of American disorder: Williams with the accumulating mass of detail in the rapidly industrializing New Jersey suburbs of New York City, Faulkner with (among other things) racial division both within individuals and among people who lived more or less together and sometimes were kin to one another. Both dealt, in different ways, with the reduction of the country's original abundance to a sum of exploitable and deteriorating "resources" for industry. They seem to have been, if not similarly, then equally burdened by their subjects—not, as with many writers, subjects sought out or acquired, but subjects that they inherited by being born in the places where they also lived their lives, and for which they were required, as a personal emergency, to find a language and an imaginative order, at the cost of a life's unremitting work and always at the risk of failure.

Such writers must accept as a working condition the risk of imperfection at best, at worst of failure. In the work of both Williams and Faulkner this risk is ever present, and the sign of it is a recurring recklessness related to desperation to "get it down" or, as Williams put it, "to say, though it be poorly / said . . ."[5] The problem for both (a problem for every writer, but perhaps especially urgent for these two) was to put down in a coherent sequence of words the tumult of details that existed simultaneously in their minds. Faulkner put it this way in "The Bear":

> . . . as the stereopticon condenses into one instantaneous field the myriad minutiae of its scope, so did that slight and rapid gesture establish in the small cramped and clut-

tered twilit room not only the ledgers but the whole plantation in its mazed and intricate entirety . . . that whole edifice intricate and complex and founded upon injustice and erected by ruthless rapacity and carried on even yet with at times downright savagery . . .[6]

Faulkner's prose, like Williams' poetry, exists absolutely in its language. To paraphrase the work of either of these writers, to explain or summarize it or otherwise render its "idea," is finally as pointless as to transform it into some sort of picture. The two have also another likeness that is significant particularly for any young would-be "follower": Their weaknesses are far more imitible than their strengths. Williams respected Faulkner for "his extraordinary sensitivity [and] a poet's use of the word," and identified with him because of his use of "good American language."[7] I don't know if he saw the resemblances that I see between Faulkner's work and his own.

Another prose writer with whom Williams felt an affinity, judging from his respectful poem to her ghost, was Marjorie Kinnan Rawlings.[8] The poem seems to refer to her autobiographical book, *Cross Creek*, which would have pleased him by its particularity and its affectionate attention to her place and its language. But for Rawlings the remote settlement of Cross Creek in Florida was a chosen place, not an inherited one. It is the fate of an inherited subject that is the basis of similarity between Williams and Faulkner. For both of them the "mass of detail" that constituted a predestined subject and trial began to accumulate before consciousness, before birth. For each the mass of local detail was the matrix from which he had to extract himself as an agent and artist consciously and conscientiously whole.

For both initially this involved the problem of finding a language that would not be merely "expressive" or "articulate" in the usual sense, but also locally appropriate. The language needed to be native to its place. There needed to be a distinct propriety between the language and its local subjects. Williams felt this need powerfully, and it explains his insistence that American writers should use the American (as opposed to the English) language, or "the American idiom." But he was wrong to imply, as he usually did, that there is *one* American language. Until we submitted our speech to the influence of radio and television, we spoke many American languages, or American variants from British English. Williams would have been clearer and sounder if he had said simply "local" instead of "American," remembering perhaps Mark Twain's note prefatory to *Huckleberry Finn*:

> In this book a number of dialects are used, to wit: the Missouri negro dialect; the extremest form of the backwoods Southwestern dialect; the ordinary "Pike County" dialect; and four modified versions of this last.

But if Williams' term was imprecise, he was nevertheless right in his insistence on the importance of local language. He

The Poetry of William Carlos Williams of Rutherford

was not doctrinaire or foolish about this. He only occasionally wrote in what might be a local dialect. Denise Levertov made the necessary point in her obituary for Williams in *The Nation*:

> Williams' poems, God knows, are not written in "the speech of Polish mothers": but he demonstrated that the poem could (and in some sense must) encompass that speech. Only a poetry with its roots in the language *as it is used* can be free to explore and reclaim all those levels that otherwise become "only literature."[9]

Perhaps she should have said, "*usually* not written in 'the speech of Polish mothers,'" for the language of some of Williams' shorter poems seems close to something he actually heard. He was seriously and delightedly attentive to the speech of his neighborhood—of, for instance, his patients. He knew that local speech gave visibility and even prominence to certain local things that "standard" speech would leave hidden. And he certainly accepted and invited this speech as an influence. It had, among other virtues, the capacity to be used with great spontaneous energy, as in this early example of which I quote only about the last third:

> This house is empty
> isn't it?
> Then it's mine
> because I need it.

Oh, I won't starve
while there's the Bible
to make them feed me.

Try to help me
if you want trouble
or leave me alone—
that ends trouble.

The county physician
is a damned fool
and you
can go to hell!

You could have closed the door
when you came in;
do it when you go out.
I'm tired.[10]

Mark Twain wrote with such care of the dialects he used because the distinctions obviously mattered to him. *Huckleberry Finn* was published in 1884, when Williams was one year old. In the 125 years since, local dialects have been subverted by media speech and homogenizing schools, and the remnants that survive are held in contempt by "the educated." For the purposes of "realism" in entertainment, we have "southern," "country," "cowboy," and a few other dialects that are as artificial and conventional as "standard American." These generally are used to mock or sentimentalize. Few now in our educational system would suspect that this loss of authentic local speech—based partly upon the familiar names of local places, people, plants, and animals; upon local weather, local topography, and local work—might be a loss, not only of cultural artifacts of interest and value, but also of a perhaps indispensable knowledge, propriety, and sensitivity. That such losses actually have happened, and that Williams was moved by an intuition fundamentally sound, is suggested by the following remarks by Ivan Illich on the music of ancient Greece:

> . . . to play music fitting for some occasion according to the rules prescribed by the ethos of Athens, one had to determine the intonation of the local flute and cithara. . . . What for us are words, the Greeks called *logoi*, or relationships. And what we understand simply as intervals between two tones would be understood as *analogia*, as the concord of the strings. This intonation had to correspond to the ethos—actually the pace, the custom, the disposition or attitude—which was as different for Dorians and Athenians as their gait and speech. . . . *Paideia*, the attuning of the common sense to the ways of a certain community, has been replaced by a universalistic education.[11]

As if in confirmation of this, my neighbor John Harrod, who applied himself to the artistry of the last of the old-time fiddlers of our region, says that fiddle tunings used to be different from one community to another—just as, before the railroads, each community set its clocks by its own particular moment of noontime.

"No Ideas But in Things"

. . . .

To confront a mass of local details, with at least the hope of bringing them to order and beauty, with the liveliest eagerness and even affection for the details, and relinquishing both the ready-made forms of traditional prosody and the omnivorous rhetoric of Whitman, was to take on a job of work extraordinarily difficult and long. Williams' need to go beyond the example of Whitman is just as significant as his need to dispense with traditional English prosody. Whitman's great trope, "Myself," was not repeatable. After Whitman, there would be little need or reason for American poets to order their work in reference to a self, either mythic or personal. For Williams, and for his purpose of a culturally useful poetry, the need was precisely opposite. The necessary reference of his work was not to his self but to his place. This called, not for a prosodic impulse or compulsion that could gather the flow of personal or poetic observations into catalogues, but for an exacting local language with which a poet on behalf of his neighbors could study, discriminate among, and put in order the particulars of an ever-accumulating "mass of detail." All at the same time, the job involved discrimination (What are the significant details? What, so far as you can see, *is* their significance?), coherence (How, so far as you can see, do the details relate to one another?), and art or "invention" (What are the means of making in a poem a coherence analogous to, and revealing, the actual coherence of the details, as far as you can see?). And this job was to be undertaken in a "provincial" place without a settled, coherent culture, or a direct and acknowledged involvement in a cultural or poetic tradition. Williams needed a language appropriate and usable, and, to give order or "measure" to the language, an appropriate and usable art of poetry. The poet's quandary and the terms of his hoped-for solution are laid out explicitly in the early pages of *Paterson*.

The purpose of that poem, as stated in the "Preface," is

> To make a start,
> out of particulars
> and make them general, rolling
> up the sum, by defective means — [1]

By "particulars" he means the "mass of detail" of the known and chosen place. By "general" he does not mean a reduction to generality by some process of averaging or abstraction, but rather an imaginative elevation to an importance generally recognizable, first by the people of Paterson and then by readers elsewhere. Local work, well done, is applicable elsewhere, not as prescription but as example. As a part of the definition of his problem, Williams recognizes as "defective means" the language and art at his disposal.

The language is "defective" because it has failed his neighbors, who also have failed it:

> They do not know the words
> or have not
> the courage to use them . . .
> . . . .
> —the language
> is divorced from their minds . . .[2]

The language fails because it is not particular enough or lively enough to deal with what must be dealt with if the people are not to remain alienated from their dwelling place and from one another—if there is to be at last an imaginative reconciliation between "the people and the stones." The required language must be capacious enough to include "the anti-poetic," not because of distaste for the poetic or a taste for the anti-poetic, but because the anti-poetic exists. To leave it out would be to ignore "half the world."[3] Besides, the needed poetry, if it is to exist, must be made poetic or beautiful by its art, not by its

"No Ideas But in Things"

subjects. To be poetic by ignoring or excluding the anti-poetic is merely to be weak. The idea of the anti-poetic, in fact, has no use or sense. The poetic is an endowment of art to subject, not from subject to art.

And so the poet of *Paterson* almost immediately rejects the possibility of making the particulars "general" by subduing or replacing them by general ideas. He sets down on page 12 and repeats with emphasis on page 18 the imperative by which his detractors most predictably belittle him, but which is probably the best brief characterization of his art and thought:

> Say it! No ideas but in things.

The conventional derogatory "interpretation" of this principle holds it to be "mindless," but it is not so except insofar as "mind" is associated with an interest in ideas apart from, or opposed to, an interest in things. Williams is speaking, on the contrary, of embodied ideas. He could have invoked in his support John 1:14 ("and the Word was made flesh, and dwelt among us . . ."). He could have, that is, if he had wished to do so, but there were good reasons not to do so, among them the numerous people to whom "the Word was made flesh" was no more than an idea. But Williams wrote at least four poems about the Nativity, two of which were about Brueghel's "The Adoration of the Kings" ("a work of art / for profound worship").[4] He, who after all was a baby doctor, understood incarnation: "a Baby / new born! / among the words."[5] When Williams denounced ideas apart from things—disembodied ideas—he was speaking as a doctor who treated his patients as individual persons, as neighbors, rather than as "cases" or "types."

He was speaking also from an ancient aversion to disconnected abstraction. Usury and inflation are two of the worst and most notorious examples of an idea (money) divorced from things (goods). Dante, as Williams would have known, put the usurers in Hell among the violent because, in defiance of Genesis 3:19, which requires us to live from nature and our work, they took "another way" (*altra via*).[6] The other way is abstraction breeding upon itself, increasing without connection to work, nature, or God. Inflation is a destabilized relation between money and goods, manipulable by the wealthy against the less wealthy, leading to an economy of "bubbles" exactly analogous to the abstract language that is manipulable by the powerful against the weak: political bubbles.

Again I think of Faulkner, whose novel *Intruder in the Dust* tells how two boys, one black and one white, and an elderly maiden lady save a black man from being lynched. They are able to do this because they respect as probable what the men of ideas dismiss as impossible. The theme or actuating principle of the novel Faulkner sets forth explicitly in the words of a minor character, a Negro man, "old Ephraim":

> *If you got something outside the common run that's got to be done and cant wait, dont waste your time on the menfolk; they works on what your uncle calls the rules and the cases. Get the womens and the children at it; they works on the circumstances.* [The italics are Faulkner's.][7]

"No Ideas But in Things"

This returns us to the issue of place as the context of work. Whether or not old Ephraim was right about the limitation of men in working "on the circumstances," his distinction is crucial, as is now increasingly apparent in the news, and his perception of the importance of circumstances is correct. In their places, the context of their local circumstances, "things" and also people escape the dominion and reduction of abstract ideas, just as a poem that refuses the separability of things and ideas resists reduction to paraphrase or "thought." Analogously, the doctor who is a neighbor who is a poet does not separate life and work, and so is never reduced to the abstract or mechanical practice of the doctor-as-specialist, who reduces healing to a profession, the patient to a vehicle for a gall bladder or an appendix, and the "doctor-patient relationship" to an "examination" that may last as little as five minutes. To Williams, his patient who was his neighbor was a case "made flesh," always in some manner an exception to the rules. He cannot follow the specialist trajectory, doing his work in ignorance of the real subject, indifferent to the circumstances, and careless of the results. The doctor who is a neighbor who is a poet is well placed to see how in the dematerializing (though materialist) modern world the individual person, place, or thing is forever disappearing into averages, statistics, and lists. But Williams does not wait with his compassion and imagination until the wagonload of abstract categories comes lumbering up. Look, for examples, at his obstetrical poem, "The Birth," and his story of another birth, "A Night in June." In "A Negro Woman," the adjective "Negro" is used as a part of the description of a particular woman, not to name her category. It is in no sense a poem about "the race problem." The woman is herself, neither more nor less, made flesh in the poet's vision and in ours.

To Williams, I think, the imagination was by definition embodied. What lies "among the words" is "a Baby / new born!" To the eye of the old baby doctor its life, in the midst of all the talk about it, is most vividly made flesh. And this comes from much further back than John 1:14. In her book on the practical agrarianism of the Bible of ancient Israel, Ellen Davis says that the difficulty of Leviticus for modern readers is that its language is "not the language of the discursive intellect, but rather that of the embodied imagination." [8] If you allow embodied thought or embodied imagination to be replaced by abstract thought, the fairly immediate result will be political and economic abstractions, reducing the living world and its creatures to quantities, rules, and cases. Such abstractions, in default of local cultures articulate and coherent enough to resist, become totally domineering and exploitive, imperial — as "backward" or "provincial" communities in Williams' time and ours, like the Jews of the Bible, have reason to know. Later in her book, Davis speaks of the wisdom of the "valorous woman" of Proverbs 31 as "a kind of intelligence bred through generations of work done in particular places, with particular materials, in response to concrete and immediate problems." This articulate, humble, practical local intelligence is antithetical to imperial rule, and it is the only effective way of resistance:

"No Ideas But in Things"

The logic of empire is centralization of information and social control; its essential processes are acculturation of local populations and appropriation of goods. Local knowledge, however, is difficult to control, since it is by definition dispersed and relatively autonomous. Nor can it be appropriated from without; [it] can be learned only from inside the community.[9]

Ivan Illich wrote that "To consider what is appropriate or fitting in a certain place leads one directly into reflection on beauty and goodness," whereas "globalization explodes any possible framework of appropriateness." Apart from local reference and the standard of local well-being, issues of economy are "reduced to numbers and utility," excluding "ethical options whose object is the good."[10] Within the framework of appropriateness, beauty, and goodness—to complete this circle— thought is embodied in the arts. Of his art of pottery, Bernard Leach wrote: "Volumes, open spaces and outlines are parts of a living whole; they are thoughts . . ." He considered the physical qualities of his work as "the breathing of the universal in the particular."[11] Edward Johnston, similarly, wrote that the craftsman "thinks in substances and in things . . . All his works express Idea (or feeling) by substance brought to life . . ."[12]

∞

It seems probable, as I suggested earlier, that Williams' concerns and even his poetry can be better authenticated and defended now than during his lifetime, but that is only because tendencies readily perceptible during his lifetime have now become so manifestly dangerous. I don't think the enlargement of these troubles would have surprised him, and it certainly removes any doubt about the pertinence and usefulness of his long struggle with problems of language and poetic form within the context of his native place.

When Williams set down plainly his manifesto, "No ideas but in things," he was not being odd or silly or unintelligent, and what he said was not unprecedented. He was accepting a limit (for himself and his own work, first of all) that would protect things from the limitlessness of abstract ideas, abstract definitions, abstract rules and cases. Things—or, by implication, persons, places, and things—properly mark the limits of ideas. Things do not merely make manifest the general names and categories by which we describe them; they also impose a discipline upon those generalities, so that the generalities do not become so general as to be unknown and unfelt in embodied particularity—so that they do not, so to speak, escape imagination and form. This is the divorce Williams speaks of early in *Paterson*: names and ideas becoming separate from the things they denote, so that "the language stutters." The tangible defines and disciplines the intangible. Concern for ideas in the absence of a concern for things, or at the expense of things, is capricious and dangerous both to things and to ideas.

For example, to make the loyalty one naturally feels for one's home or one's native countryside into an abstract nationalism is to produce an emotion that is formless: out of control.

Nationalists are people out of control. They seek, not the good of their country, peculiar to it, hence not conflicting with the good of any other country, but rather the dominance of an idea of patriotism in ready subservience to political ambition. This idea, cut loose from the actual ground, is without tangible limit. Nationalists are at liberty, given sufficient power, to subjugate either their neighbors or the world. Far from the implicit restraints of Williams' subordination of ideas to things, nationalists find it easy to countenance the destruction of innocent people and creatures, and of the world itself, for the sake of ideas.

An idea so abstract is readily subverted by a "national economy" or a "global economy" of corporations using money (an idea divorced from things of actual value) to expropriate the people and exploit (and destroy) the land. The country thus comes piecemeal under their dominion. Williams' "genius" was not in seeing that this is true so much as in placing himself where he could not help but see it. Anybody who in the age of industrialism makes common cause with a place, and who looks, will see that it is always under threat of damage or destruction for the sake of money. Against the "tribe" to whom nothing in particular matters as much as its price, who will destroy anything for the right price, Williams posed the authentic local economy of Brueghel's peasants, whose clothes "were of better stuff, hand woven, than we can boast." [13] A number of times Williams refers to peasants or "peasant traditions," not out of sentimentality or an interest in folklore, but because they represented a kind of culture, authentically local and self-sustaining, that could protect even the poor from exploitation by an economy gone crazy.

There are several such instances of runaway ideas that our own time has exaggerated into obviousness. For another example, the instinct that we have decided to call "sexuality" has become a generalized socioeconomic idea, not to be limited by association with any particular person, deity, or institution, and therefore usable by merchants as a kind of bait. Hunger, as Michael Pollan has shown, has likewise become a commercial idea, dissociated from health or bodily need and only tentatively related to food.[14] The world itself has become an engulfing idea, known to conservationists, politicians, corporations, advertisers, and others as "the environment," thereby obliterating local names, memories, and stories along with the patterns of their association. Without a conventional or habitual willingness to divorce ideas from things, people would not call their home places or their home planet "the environment."

"No ideas but in things," the good Dr. Williams insisted, and we see more clearly every day how rightly he did so. In his late work, he saw the nuclear bomb as the perfectly apt symbol, as it is the perfectly illustrative example, of an idea released from the limits of things, an idea unrestrained by respect for any thing. It is itself of course a thing, but it is the oddest of things: a perfect materialization of an abstract idea, a thing whose only purpose is the destruction of everything. It is the ultimate idol:

· 55

The mere picture
of the exploding bomb
fascinates us
so that we cannot wait
to prostrate ourselves
before it.[15]

The bomb is exactly opposite to love, to imagination, to poetry, to beauty. In our own country, the "flower" discovered for Europe by Columbus, we are said to have 12,000 nuclear warheads. By what power may we oppose them? Only a language, only a poetry, as Williams would have said, by which to know, to imagine and cherish, the things we have become officially willing to destroy. Otherwise: "The bomb speaks."[16] *Only* the bomb speaks. To imagine, to speak of and for, the things, persons, and places by which we actually live is to break the carapace of official identity and general ideas. It is to talk back to the bomb, to all it stands for, and with some hope of effect.

A Matter
of Necessity

. . . .

To rescue ourselves, our fellow beings, and our places from the rampage of big ideas that feed upon without recognizing all the things of the world, we need an adequate language—a language not alienated from us by divorce from things and therefore at the service of our exploiters and oppressors. We need at the very least a speakable inventory of the things particularly belonging to our own places and lives that are worth saving. First of all we must rescue our language from the generalizers, the categorizers, the classifiers, the reducers of things to ideas, the mongers of stereotypes and clichés, the "clerks" of the universities who, Williams says in *Paterson*, have got out of hand, forgetting for the most part to whom they are beholden:

>   spitted on fixed concepts like
>   roasting hogs, sputtering, their drip sizzling
>   in the fire [1]

That is harsh, but in view of all that is at stake it may not be too harsh. Since it was written it has become more just, for the universities have by principle deracinated the arts and the sciences in the service of what Ivan Illich called "universalistic education." They have promoted, fallaciously and at great costs, the idea that there is one universal solution for every local problem. (By this idea alone the land grant universities have undercut their mandated purpose and betrayed their legally designated constituencies.) They have become the no-places of disembodied thought, where the typical deception, beginning apparently with self-deception, is the substitution of ideas, or merely names, for things. I have in mind not only their succumbing to "the intellectual temptation of substituting vocabulary for thought," to borrow a useful diagnosis from John Lukacs,[2] but also their orientation of thought to the capabilities of technology, from machines to chemicals to genetic engineering, rather than to the nature and ecological limits of places. Universities, great and small, have thus become the sources of novelty but not of originality in the necessarily particular and local sense of that term. To the academic professionals, any local loyalty or the adoption of local well-being as a standard of work would seem "provincial" and beneath notice. They have generated an epidemic of specialized or professional languages that are ugly, intentionally obscure, pretentious, and incapable of particularity, affection, humility, or wonder. These languages are readily usable for commercial and political lies, and are sometimes taught at public expense for that purpose.

The survival of poetry, in fact the survival of humans and their world, depends upon the cultivation of better language. Williams was right: The universities were not in his time, and they still are not, offering themselves as places for such cultivation.

To Williams, the need for an adequate language, lively and exact to serve us rather than our exploiters, is linked inextricably to our need for an adequate art of language, which is to say an adequate poetry. To have both was for Williams a necessity of the greatest urgency. How else confront, "interrelate," bring to order, even to beauty, how else imagine and put within reach of love the always accumulating "mass of detail"? A passage of dialogue in "The Desert Music" starts with a question, obviously amusing to Williams, that leads him to declare his motive with stark seriousness:

> You seem quite normal. Can you tell me? Why
> does one want to write a poem?
>
> Because it's there to be written.
>
> Oh. A matter of inspiration then?
>
> Of necessity.

A Matter of Necessity

Oh. But what sets it off?

> I am he whose brains
> are scattered
>   aimlessly [3]

The last lines no doubt refer to the stroke that had come shortly before this poem. But of course everybody's brains, by nature and circumstances, are scattered aimlessly; if the mind is to be orderly it must be *made* orderly. Williams' reply, "Of necessity," is at once personal and cultural, and also deliberately ambiguous. Poems worthy of the name, and of the effort to make them, are made of necessity by inspiration and because they are needed. But if we are to have them, we must have a way of making them: an art.

æ **8** æ

Two Mysteries:
Inspiration
and Talent

. . . .

To the extent that we can usefully speak of it, an art must be conscious; it must be something that an artist deliberately learns to do and deliberately does. But we are immediately in difficulty, for the conscious portion of an art is never all, and may not be even half. Our consciousness of an art, our effort to understand and explain it, is baffled on the one hand by the mystery of inspiration, and on the other by the mystery of talent.

Why would a normal person want to write a poem? Williams seems to have enjoyed the question. I enjoy it too, and I assume for the same reason: the jumpiness it puts into that word "normal." Williams does seem to have been a fairly normal fellow, if by that we mean that he was in charge of himself, did his work, and was liked by a lot of people, evidently by a lot of different kinds of people. But he was abnormal as a person, though normal as a poet, in acknowledging the reality of inspiration. He would want to write a poem, he says at first, "because it's there to be written." His questioner understands him: "A matter of inspiration then?" But at that point Williams dodges, giving a second answer that is different, though also true: "Of necessity." He dodges, probably, for two reasons. He has thought both of his great need at that time to survive his illness *as a poet* and of the great general need for poetry that he speaks of in a famous and maybe too often quoted passage in "Asphodel, That Greeny Flower"[1]—he is defending his art. But he dodges also, I think, because he did not want his questioner to ask him how it was that for an apparently "quite normal" person a poem should be "there to be written." He couldn't explain inspiration, and he didn't want to be asked to do so. Later, in "Asphodel, That Greeny Flower," having no "normal" questioner to fend off, he speaks of

> the words
> made solely of air
> or less,
> that came to me
> out of the air
> and insisted
> on being written down.[2]

The Poetry of William Carlos Williams of Rutherford

He probably could have said it no better and no more plainly. Nobody can account for inspiration. Like all who have experienced it, Williams was grateful for it, knowing he needed all the help he could get. Philip Guston was referring to inspiration, I think, when he wrote to Ross Feld in 1978 of

the <u>generous law</u> that exists in art. A law which can never be given but only found anew each time in the making of the work . . . The only problem is how to keep away from the minds that close in and itch (God knows why) to define it.[3]

An even more difficult aspect of this mystery of inspiration is the sense that a poem is reaching beyond itself, beyond what one has known to put in it and what it has been able to include, toward something more. Williams referred explicitly to this in a letter he wrote in 1954 to Denise Levertov about a poem she had sent to him:

After all a poem is made up not of the things of which it speaks directly but of things which it cannot identify and yet yearns to know. You have brushed the raiments of an unknown host in these lines.[4]

It is pleasing to suppose Levertov was remembering that letter when she wrote eighteen years later about Williams' poem, "The Sound of Waves," which ends:

Two Mysteries: Inspiration and Talent

Past that, past the image:
a voice!
out of the mist
above the waves and

the sound of waves, a
voice   .   speaking! [5]

To Levertov this poem suggested

> a poetics inseparable from the rest of human experience
> and—*not* because of its content but by its very nature,
> its forms, its sensuous forms that are its very essence—
> expresses and defines the nature of humanness; and in
> so doing arrives at the edge of the world, where all is
> unknown, undefined, the abyss of the gods. [6]

Thus both Williams and Levertov testify to a prayer-like
reaching-beyond that may be indigenous to all art worth the
name. And this is not the same as the reaching of modern science;
it has nothing to do with "the cutting edge." What is being
reached for is by definition suggestable but not realizable in
art; it certainly cannot be verified by facts or corroborated by
experimentation. This reaching is valuable because, like prayer,
it grants a necessary amplitude to our nature and experience. It
is therefore one of the reasons for including the arts in education. Implicit in this thought of "reaching" is the apparent fact

that language at its best is, as much as numbers, inherently a reductive medium. We live within and from a reality that we cannot know in full by any of our systems of knowing. And this is a limitation conventionally and dangerously ignored by the arts and sciences both.

I have said that Williams' poems mean what they say, and that what they say is the only way of saying what they mean. I have said also that they engage in a sort of conversation with the details of local life and circumstances, which implies that they may mean more than they say, as they are enlarged by connections that radiate from them. And now I have added the thought, Williams' thought, that they may be further enlarged by gestures or reachings-out toward a reality that they cannot directly express. I don't think I am at cross-purposes here. A poem may without contradiction say what it means, mean what it says, mean more than it says, and say more than the poet meant it to say. I am to some extent a literalist: I like plain-speaking in a poem, and if something can be said plainly I don't think it gains in artistic value by being said obscurely. But because of the complexity of its relation to its origin, its subject, and the circumstances within which it was written and is read, every good poem has its own perimeter of obscurity. Within a somewhat larger perimeter this obscurity may be clarified by insight and discussion, but at a boundary still further the obscurity becomes authentically mysterious, and there inquiry needs to stop. An indispensable propriety of explanation is in knowing when to stop. Inspiration as a subject of interest and

Two Mysteries: Inspiration and Talent

inquiry thus has a certain standing, granted to it by poets who have testified both to its necessity and to its mystery. We can speak of it a little, but not much.

⚭

About the mystery of talent there seems to be less to say than about the mystery of inspiration. Every passage of his poetry that I have quoted, like hundreds that I have not quoted, suggests that Williams had a talent specifically for the making of words into poems. Here, for another example, is "Nantucket":

> Flowers through the window
> lavender and yellow
>
> changed by white curtains—
> Smell of cleanliness—
>
> Sunshine of late afternoon—
> On the glass tray
>
> a glass pitcher, the tumbler
> turned down, by which
>
> a key is lying—And the
> immaculate white bed[7]

In a letter to me on March 5, 2001, Donald Hall wrote: "Why is it that something like 'Nantucket' can shine in the dark of the night?" The question ought to be asked, but Mr. Hall rightly did not try to answer it. I doubt that anybody with much sense would try to answer it. Literary industrialists probably could heap up explanations around it, for that is their job, but they would only make a murk through which this poem would continue quietly to shine.

The mystery of talent ought to be (but usually is not) taken as fair warning by those who try to found a literary politics on traditional or nontraditional verse forms. If you have no talent, studying his prosody and observing the mass of urban detail will not make you as good a poet as William Carlos Williams, just as studying traditional prosody and going to church will not make you as good a poet as George Herbert. Neither attempt will make you even a passable verse-writer, if you have no talent. That is merely to say that technical knowledge in any amount cannot be satisfactorily substituted for the ability to *hear* the difference between a good line and a bad one. Williams, like Herbert, had an excellent ear, and his use of it in writing his poems was acute. Donald Davie could hardly have been more wrong in saying that "Williams had a pictorial, not an auditory, sensibility." [8]

Two Mysteries: Inspiration and Talent

Art Conscious
and Learnable

. . . .

Between the great mysteries of inspiration and talent, always qualified by them and yet necessary, is the conscious art of poetry that can be deliberately learned and practiced by poets and by readers. But here is another qualification we need to remember: That an art is to some extent conscious and learnable does not mean always that what is known can be reduced to rules or even expressed in language. Accomplished artists will probably have their lists of dos and don'ts, but some knowledge must be communicated by examples.

There are two ways, so far as I can see, in which we can become conscious of the presence of art, a way of making, in a piece of writing. First is the necessity, which I mentioned earlier, of rendering into a sequential order of words the many details or thoughts that exist simultaneously in the mind. For this reason alone writing can never be a copy of reality. Simultaneity of knowledge or consciousness can be made sequential only artificially: by art. If, for example, I should undertake to write a simple prose description of my window's "view" of several species of trees, a river, and distant hills, I would have to make many decisions about what to include and when or where to include it. If I did this in such a way as to give this scene something like the sense of visibility in a reader's mind that it has in my own, the reader might reasonably conclude that I possess an adequate art of writing. But if I produced something hard to read, arranging the details in no sensible order, giving no vision to the reader's mind, then the reader might decide with justice that, having no art, I made only a mess. A reader who could compare two such pieces and see intelligently the differences between them would know something about art.

That is a reasonable way of knowing. The other way is that of experience. Suppose, for a second example, that you are a young person who would like to be a poet, and you read "January Morning," a fairly early poem by William Carlos Williams. You see how his vision has come so lively and freshly—so visibly—to the pages. How simple and straightforward it is! "Surely," you think, "I can do that. All I have to do is see what is happening and write it down in lines as Williams did." His lines, you decide, since they don't scan according to any named foot, are in "free" verse. But then you try to write such a poem for yourself, and you discover that you cannot do it. If you had hoped to write a good poem, you are disappointed. If you are at all intelligent, however, your disappointment is not wasted, for it has taught you something: Art is involved. If you want to write well, you will have to learn how. This would have been obvious to you if you were making your first attempt to use a welding torch or play the violin, but one of the dangers of poetry, since most people are more or less literate, is that a good poem can look easy. But now you know that when Williams wrote "January Morning," he was using an art he had learned, perhaps by way of much effort, much failure and disappointment. If you then get *The Collected Poems*, Volume I, and read the hundred pages of poems that precede "January Morning," you'll find work that, compared to that poem, is not so good. You will find admirable poems also, but you may reasonably suspect that the poet worked his way to each new poem partly by the motive of disappointment with the last.

How are we to understand the conscious art of poetry well enough to talk intelligently about it? I have had to confess my inability to make much sense or use of Williams' theory of "the variable foot." I confess this reluctantly and with the hope that the failure is mine, but the problem remains. The variable foot was a product, maybe useful to him, of Williams' effort to rationalize his instinctive rejection of the iambic foot as a metrical norm. I see no reason to say that he was wrong in this. Any prosodic choice, like a choice of any other kind, is necessarily exclusive. In order to do anything, you must choose one way and reject all others. If the speech—the way of *talking*—of your neighbors matters to you and you would like to accept its influence in your poetry, then you will have to discard the iamb as a norm.

But Williams' rejection, doctrinaire as it may have been, was not absolute. The iambic line, whether your language is British or American, has a rhetorical energy that, when the speech grows lyrical or the tone conclusive, may be irresistible. Williams returns to it repeatedly even in poems most conscientiously written in the variable foot:

> The light
>
> for all time shall outspeed
>
> the thunder crack.[1]

To make as much sense as I am able, I would like to carry the question of the art of poetry to what seem to me to be the fundamentals. Since the subject of "prose poetry" is largely without relevance to Williams, and is a source of much confusion to me, I am going to say for present purposes — with all due respect to prose, prose poems, and poetic prose — that poetry distinguishes itself from prose by being written in lines.

Line and
Syntax

. . . .

If it were not for the necessity of being written or printed on pages and the convention of paragraphing, a work in prose would continue straight ahead, like the line in the middle of a road, to the final period. A line of poetry, by contrast, ends short of the right-hand margin of the page. It ends at a place chosen by the poet. Even such long lines as Whitman's, which often exceed the width of the page and so are turned back arbitrarily at the edge, finally reach a point at which they end by the poet's choice.

If one line ends at a chosen place, the beginning of the next line also is determined by choice. A line of poetry therefore has two points, a beginning and an end, that are not arbitrary but are chosen. Every line of verse, traditionally formed or not, is formed by the choice of the poet, and is to that extent free. But because the choice is made, and is made for reasons that exclude other reasons, every line is deliberately limited, and in that sense it is not free.

Williams therefore was right to reject the notion of "free verse," for there is no escaping the limitations of a choice, however freely made, once it is made. The only question then is of the significance of the choice. I suppose, further, that the significance may be determined by the complexity of concerns that govern the choice.

If a line of poetry has a determined beginning and end, then this implies a movement, a forward movement that the skilled poet also will be aware of and able to control. Made with sufficient skill, a line can move quickly or slowly, with lesser or greater force, or it can be stopped somewhere between beginning and end and then allowed to continue. These mid-line interruptions occur typically when the coherence of the line comes under stress from the coherence of sense. A line is interrupted usually when it is required to accommodate a sentence ending or a syntactical pause.

වෙ

To say that poetry distinguishes itself from prose by being written in lines is not at all to suggest that poetry need not concern itself with sentences, or that sentences are less important than lines. It seems to me that in the poems I like best the two structural members, line and sentence, are of equal importance. The line, I think, has the character of music, and the sentence or syntax the character of sense. The expressive means of poetry thus consists not only of the play of line against line and of sentence against sentence, but of the interplay of line and sentence.

One can readily see, for example, the nearly perfect (and rather passive) coincidence of line and syntax in Shakespeare's Sonnet 73 —

> That time of year thou mayst in me behold
> When yellow leaves, or none, or few, do hang
> Upon those boughs which shake against the cold,
> Bare ruined choirs where late the sweet birds sang.

—as compared with Sonnet 129, in which the syntax presses with extraordinary force against the structure both of the lines and the quatrain:

> Th' expense of spirit in a waste of shame
> Is lust in action; and, till action, lust
> Is perjured, murd'rous, bloody, full of blame,
> Savage, extreme, rude, cruel, not to trust . . .

In considering the interaction of line and syntax one begins to see how crude a tool traditional scansion is. Without it, Robert Frost said, writing poetry is like playing tennis without a net. Maybe so, but the net is only rudimentary; you might be able to hit the ball over the net and still be a bad player. When Donne wrote "The Good-Morrow,"

Line and Syntax

> I wonder, by my troth, what thou and I
> Did, till we loved? Were we not weaned till then . . . ,

he of course knew he was writing in iambic pentameter; the line-form serves the poem in ways that are obvious, and it may have served the making of the poem in ways we don't know. Knowing the meter of the poem may be of some help to a reader, but not much. What the reader will respond to, consciously or not, is the way the lines divide the syntax and the way the syntax in turn divides the lines. The poem is shaped, and its quality determined, by this reciprocity far more than by the line form or meter.

Likewise, much of the power of Milton's sonnet on his blindness, "When I consider how my light is spent," is made by the suspension of sense and syntax over the endings of the first thirteen lines, line and syntax becoming perfectly concordant, bringing the poet and his poem to rest, only in the final line:

> They also serve who only stand and wait.

Williams understood well, and understood better as his life and poetic practice lengthened, this potency of the relation between line and syntax. He was, as we know also from his prose, an excellent writer of sentences. Yvor Winters praised highly the prose of "The Destruction of Tinochtitlan" (the third essay of *In the American Grain*), and surely he did so because of such passages as this:

Streets, public squares, markets, temples, palaces, the city spread its dark life upon the earth of a new world, rooted there, sensitive to its richest beauty, but so completely removed from those foreign contacts which harden and protect, that at the very breath of conquest it vanished. The whole world of its unique associations sank back into the ground to be reënkindled, never. Never, at least save in spirit . . . [1]

One notices here not just the syntax, so powerfully and beautifully formed, but also the way these sentences illuminate the word "conquest" and its influence on our history to this day.

During my student years, *Poetry* magazine carried a series of endorsements by noted poets. Of these, the letter from Williams, dated February 21, 1955, was by far the best:

Without POETRY the poem like the wild pigeon would have remained among us no more than an official memory.

This was the only one of those statements that I remembered word for word without even trying. It shows how almost naturally, and how much for pleasure, Williams could write a perfectly balanced sentence. This one, though it takes up, as if from the essay just quoted, the theme of extinction, which seems to have haunted him as it now haunts many of us, is even so a piece of exuberant hyperbole. He was enjoying himself.

In his poetry Williams seems to me to be most assured, and his poems most satisfactory, when line and syntax are most actively collaborating. I will offer two examples. This is from "The Yachts":

> Mothlike in mists, scintillant in the minute
>
> brilliance of cloudless days, with broad bellying sails
> they glide to the wind tossing green water
> from their sharp prows while over them the crew
> crawls
>
> ant-like, solicitously grooming them, releasing,
> making fast as they turn, lean far over and having
> caught the wind again, side by side, head for the
> mark.[2]

My next example is the whole of "The Cure," which records a small triumph on the part of a self-doubting "provincial" poet. The poem, in both "plot" and syntax, moves from anxiety to resolution in a way that may remind one of Milton's sonnet on his blindness, the hesitant short sentences giving way to a confident and finally joyous long one:

Sometimes I envy others, fear them
a little too, if they write well.
For when I cannot write I'm a sick man
and want to die. The cause is plain.

But they have no access to my sources.
Let them write then as they may and
perfect it as they can they will never
come to the secret of that form

interknit with the unfathomable ground
where we walk daily and from which
among the rest you have sprung
and opened flower-like to my hand.[3]

Williams must have been surprised, and tickled, to find that he
had written a poem that turned out to be a love poem to itself.
Doubt of his gift and his vocation seems to have been often
with him. Could he, while others of greater reputation lived
in centers of culture abroad, become a significant poet of the
peripheral small cities where he walked daily? He was brave
enough to ask, and he was gifted and accomplished enough
to be answered by his work. We feel his exhilaration when
the energy of that long sentence comes to him and he plays
it out, submitting to the checks and inflections of the lines.
The poem, though not traditionally formal, is nonetheless perfectly formed. Hear, for example, how "and" of the hardly

conventional line, "Let them write as they may and," chimes with "can" in the next line, is echoed by two more "ands," and then is rhymed with "hand," the final word of the poem, for a perfect close. The poem attains an added eloquence from its resonance with other uses by Williams of the image of an opening flower.

๛ **11** ๛

The
Three-Part
Line

. . . .

Later Williams invented, as he would have put it, what
I suppose we can call rightly enough a three-part line:

> The descent beckons
> > as the ascent beckoned
> > > Memory is a kind
> of accomplishment
> > a sort of renewal
> > > even
> an initiation . . .[1]

This formal device he first used in the passage whose beginning
lines I have just quoted; it is from Book Two of *Paterson*, published in 1948. He used it also in "The Problem," published in a

magazine in 1953 but not in a book until *The Collected Poems*, volume II. He used it for most of *The Desert Music* of 1954, all of *Journey to Love* of 1955; also in "On St. Valentine's Day" and "The Birth," neither of which was published in a book until *The Collected Poems*, volume II; in several passages of Book Five of *Paterson*; and in "The Gift" and "The Turtle" in *Pictures from Breughel*. Toward the end of his life, Williams' interest in his three-part line seems to have slackened. I doubt that this can be definitively explained, but I would guess that it had become too much and too noticeably a *set* form, too predictable. Or maybe he got tired of it. But while his excitement with it lasted, it gave him the most eloquent and moving, and the most consistently vital of all his poems.

In the poems in which he used the three-part line, and out of his long ardor and experience, he spoke at length, in a sort of vigilantly particularizing discourse, of the things that concerned him most and that ought most to concern us all: of suffering, disorder, disintegration, the nuclear bomb, but also of forgiveness, love, beauty, worship, and of the ordering and clarifying power of imagination, its indispensable ability to make real what otherwise is lost "at the very breath of conquest." Nowhere else in his work, I think, are there so many or such lovely cooperations of line and syntax. The visual spacings of the line breaks, thrusting into the momentum of the syntax, act as a sort of musical notation much more explicit and sensitive than traditional scansion. These poems offer one passage after another as articulate as a conductor's wrist. Here is one from "The Artist":

> Mr. T.
> > bareheaded
> > > in a soiled undershirt
> > his hair standing out
> > > on all sides
> > > > stood on his toes
> > heels together
> > > arms gracefully
> > > > for the moment
> > curled above his head.
> > > Then he whirled about
> > > > bounded
> > into the air
> > > and with an *entrechat*
> > > > perfectly achieved
> > completed the figure.[2]

It is impossible to imagine the hardness of critical principle that could resist the humor and the grace of that.

And here, by contrast, and illustrative of the versatility of this line form, is a passage in which he returns — conceptually — to the inadequacy of concepts and therefore the necessity of imagination. The movement here, explicitly, is from concept to imagination:

> Ripped from the concept of our lives
> > and from all concept
> > > somehow, and plainly,

the sun will come up
　　　　each morning
　　　　　　　and sink again.
So that we experience
　　　　violently
　　　　　　　every day
two worlds
　　　　one of which we share with the
　　　　rose in bloom
　　　　　　　and one,
by far the greater,
　　　　with the past,
　　　　　　　the world of memory,
the silly world of history,
　　　　the world
　　　　　　　of the imagination.
. . . .
　　　　　　　The instant
trivial as it is
　　　　is all we have
　　　　　　　unless—unless
things the imagination feeds upon,
　　　　the scent of the rose,
　　　　　　　startle us anew.[3]

"The silly world of history"? History strictly of the past tense, reduced to fact, without the kindling of the imagination to which, as Faulkner said and as Williams would have agreed, the past is not past.

And here, by contrast again, is a memory, a story, a piece of history, called back by imagination into presence, a sudden clarity in the midst of a general vagueness. It is from the splendid love poem, "Asphodel, That Greeny Flower":

> Do you remember
> > how at Interlaken
> > > we were waiting, four days,
> to see the Jungfrau
> > but rain had fallen steadily.
> > > > Then
> just before train time
> > on a tip from one of the waitresses
> > > we rushed
> to the Gipfel Platz
> > and there it was!
> > > in the distance
> covered with new-fallen snow.[4]

So strong was Williams' proclivity and talent for sentence-making that its influence is active and is felt as a shaping force even in poems in which the syntax is fragmented and the sentences incomplete. His sense of line is equally powerful and equally felt even when he is using the line to thwart our sense of the logic of syntax or our expectation that a line of poetry will be in itself rhythmically coherent. These two elements of composition, line and sentence, if taken seriously and used intelligently, by their interplay become strongly formal, mitigate against garrulousness, and so take us far both from "free" verse and from the fast (and ill-formed) "communication" that is the modern ideal. The collaboration of line and sentence is both a restraint that makes for considered speech and an impetus that moves speech toward music.

&

Williams' renunciation of any ready-made ideal of formal perfection may seem sometimes to make him vulnerable to detractors who accused him of carelessness. He did at times publish two versions of a poem, one clearly better than the other. But this apparent carelessness, in fact, provides as good evidence as we need that his formation of his art was *not* careless. There is much to be said, I think, for the idea that a poet should publish a poem in its single best version. We know, however, that revision after publication is hardly unheard-of. Fortunately for defenders of his work, Williams published two versions of the beginning of "Asphodel, That Greeny Flower."

The first, obviously a fragment, entitled "Paterson, Book V: The River of Heaven," was published in *Poetry* in 1952. I will quote about half of it:

> Of asphodel, that greeny flower, the least,
> that is a simple flower

> like a buttercup upon its
> branching stem, save
> that it's green and wooden
> We've had a long life
> and many things have happened in it.
> There are flowers also
> in hell. So today I've come
> to talk to you about them, among
> other things, of flowers . . .⁵

This version clearly is a failure, falling short of the standard even of decent prose, and just as clearly it is a failure of form. It falters both in line and syntax. Williams, as he himself might have put it, has not found the measure.

By 1954, when this passage, transformed, was published as the beginning of "Work in Progress" in *The Desert Music*, Williams *has* found the measure. The lines move with a musical integrity that is maintained to the end:

> Of asphodel, that greeny flower,
> like a buttercup
> upon its branching stem—
> save that it's green and wooden—
> I come, my sweet,
> to sing to you.
> We lived long together
> a life filled,
> if you will,

with flowers. So that
            I was cheered
                    when I came first to know
that there were flowers also
                    in hell.[6]

❧ **12** ❧

Economy
and Form

. . . .

  I need to speak of two other fundamental principles that are formal—or, more accurately, principles that are economic and therefore formal. These are principles that I think Williams carefully observed. The first is this: When what is to be said has been said, stop. This applies to all speaking and writing, but it applies most urgently to poetry. If you don't know where to stop, you don't know what your subject is, and likely you won't know, or find out, where to start. There is nothing so discouraging as the feeling that what is being written or said or read or heard could go on and on without limit.

  The second principle, obviously related to the first, is this: Say only what needs to be said. In his introduction to *The Wedge* of 1944, in contradiction of one of my own principles and much to my dislike, Williams said, "A poem is a small (or large) machine made of words."[1] In the years between 1944 and now, that metaphor of the machine has grown upon us until it has ceased to be a metaphor and has become an equation or an identity, so that organisms, including ourselves and our minds and the world itself, are now conventionally spoken of as machines, and this has helped to make us cold-hearted and destructive. But Williams' explanation of his metaphor is perfectly acceptable to me: He meant, as he went on to say, that a poem, like a machine, should have no redundant parts. It should not be overloaded. He is speaking practically. A robin does not need four feet or a long bushy tail. You can't transport a cow in a wheelbarrow. A line, a sentence, or a poem can have its back broken by too many details or too many words. There is pleasure, and there is beauty too, in any work accomplished with an exacting sense of enough.

Here, for example, is "The Term":

> A rumpled sheet
> of brown paper
> about the length
>
> and apparent bulk
> of a man was
> rolling with the
>
> wind slowly over
> and over in
> the street as

a car drove down
upon it and
crushed it to

the ground. Unlike
a man it rose
again rolling

with the wind over
and over to be as
it was before.[2]

It is easy to see how an unwary young imitator could mistake
this for free verse, simple and easy. It certainly is not pretentious. Nobody could call it magnificent. But if we are not an
unwary young imitator, we begin our second thoughts about
the poem when we feel its considerable power. Its power comes
from its overturning of expectations. At first we may think we
are reading a poem that is merely descriptive or "imagist." By
the end of the fourth stanza, we may suspect that the poem is
developing a metaphor. But the metaphor, "the length // and
apparent bulk / of a man," turns out to be a sort of reverse
simile: "Unlike / a man it rose / again . . ." It becomes a poem
about the finality with which a man can be crushed by a machine.
Quietly, without breaking stride, the poem assumes poignance
and gravity dramatically disproportionate to its occasion.

The occasion of this poem is small, without any significance that is immediately apparent. It is odd, too. I suppose this is an instance of the "anti-poetic." But the image of the blowing paper does not shock us by being anti-poetic. It shocks us by becoming suddenly poetic—and a lot more poetic than we expected. What the unwary imitator needs to see is that the poem's sudden access of power is made possible by its strict economy, which may register on our senses at first merely as unpretentiousness. But not a word is wasted. Excess at any point would have spoiled everything. The short lines involve a considerable risk, for each must contribute substantially to the poem in only two or three words, and they must in no way obstruct its movement. This risk could hardly have been ignored by the poet. It is forthrightly addressed, and is surmounted with consummate skill. The lines are precisely, delicately—beautifully—weighted as they suspend the syntax to the end first of a long sentence, and then to the end of a shorter but more telling one.

Measure

. . . .

In speaking of economy I have begun to speak of measure, as one would expect. Williams insisted on the importance of measure, and he was right. But "measure," especially in speaking of poetry but often also in general use, is a tricky term. It is perfectly dependable when it refers to the size of a material object, but it is not so dependable when used in reference to the length or duration of a line of poetry. Often in poetry what is being measured is not so substantial even as words; sometimes we are measuring silence, as in a pause within a line or between lines or between stanzas. That is why the "variable foot"—or any other kind of foot—is of little use in understanding or explaining the artistic quality of a poem.

Another difficulty of "measure" is its way of sliding almost imperceptibly from literal to figurative sense. When I said that "The Term" moves into its significance "without breaking stride," I was speaking of measure in the literal sense: I was talking about rhythm. But when I spoke of its lines as "precisely weighted," I was allowing my term of measurement to become more metaphorical than literal. When I said that the lines are not so weighted as to impede the movement of the poem, I was speaking again of measure in the sense of rhythm, but the lines of course are weighted *as if* carefully weighed.

And so "measure" may refer to an actually measured quantity, such as a counted rhythm or a number of syllables, or, as in the phrase "in measure," it can mean "carefully considered." In poetry the sense of careful consideration may be given by the rhythmical deliverance line by line of what is being said, as a rope may be paid out rhythmically hand over hand. It is felt partly as an auditory suggestion that the poet is listening, and thus asking the reader to listen, carefully to what is being said.

Williams returned repeatedly to the issue of measure. To him, concern for measure seems to have been nearly synonymous with concern for the art of poetry. Measured verse was artful or "made,"[1] in contrast to verse that was artless or "free." He was driven by the prevalent mischief of free verse to insist that "you cannot be / an artist / by mere ineptitude."[2] And he wrote to Richard Eberhart on October 23, 1953, that

> there can be no absolute freedom in verse. You must have a measure but a relatively expanded measure to exclude what has to be excluded and to include what has to be included. It is a technical point but a point of vast importance.[3]

As frequently in reading Williams on technique, I am partly baffled by this. I don't know what he meant by "a relatively expanded measure" — and so, when I speak of measure, I will be relying on my own understanding of the term.

Otherwise, I think his statement to Eberhart *is* of vast importance. Concern for measure rises apparently from respect for limits. It thus involves an issue that is only in part technical. To speak "in measure" is to speak with a proper respect for art, but it is also to speak with a proper, and therefore limiting, respect for what you are saying and where and to whom you are saying it. It is to speak willingly within formal limits, but it is also to speak with propriety in the fullest, best sense of that term. "Any old way" will not do. To speak in measure is therefore to reject the esthetic of "anything goes," which is concordant with the industrial economic ethic of profit from anything at any cost.

In poetry, as in our economic life, the phrase "in measure" serves notice that some things may be properly included, but not everything or anything. Or we can say, as we would say of a field or a farm, that a poem has a certain carrying capacity. If that capacity is exceeded, the poem stumbles or breaks down. If, on the other hand, the poem is not overburdened, and if it is otherwise well-handled, it will have a margin of ease in which it can move fluently — and maybe this gives us a practical, an auditory, sense of "in measure." What has been included is brought within measure, made eloquent, even musical, by being freed of the burden of all that has been, has needed to be, excluded.

The question of measure in the strict or quantitative sense brings us directly, as Williams understood, to the question, or rather to the many questions, of the musical nature of poetry. If we assume that lyric poetry began as song, as songs sung to a lyre, and that epic or narrative poetry originally was chanted or intoned, then we may have to assume also that it is dangerous if not fatal for a poem to stray too far from music, too far toward language that is merely "free." We may suspect that poetry is valuable as such because of its ability to bring our language near to music. Without music, vision or power or revelation or honesty or intelligence or learning or fact or shocking fact may be of interest but will not make a poem. "It don't mean a thing if it ain't got that swing."[4] Williams wrote again on this subject to Richard Eberhart on May 23, 1954. And again I fail to make sense of everything in the letter, but I understand what I'm about to quote, and it is useful. First he says, "I have never been one to write by rule, even by my own rules." There is both relief and pleasure in the candor of that, and it is fair warning. It seems right to me that practice should take precedence over theory, and Williams seems to have given it a calculated permission to do so. He then says that "the rule of counted syllables . . . has become tiresome to my ear." He says this so quietly here that we need to remind ourselves how fiercely he rejected the traditional metrics. His concern is nevertheless with the necessity of measure: "the stated syllables, as in the best of present-day free verse, have become entirely divorced from the beat, that is the measure." A little further on he says, "By measure I mean musical pace."[5] Later in the same letter he uses the word "beat" to mean a single stress given in no specified place to each part of his three-part line, and I simply am stumped by this. But in the sentences I have quoted I believe that by "the beat" and "measure" he means rhythm, and in general I think he was more observant of the rhythms of his poems than of his rules.

❧ **14** ❧

Rhythm

· ·

  In talking about the music of poetry, I think it is better to begin with rhythm than with line measurement by numbers of syllables or feet. It is not hard to find two perfectly iambic lines—let us say the first lines of Shakespeare's sonnets 73 and 129, which I quoted in chapter 10—that have different rhythms. By "rhythm" I mean the beat or tempo to which a poem is read. The rhythm would be consonant with and would denote the mood or tone of the poem. Both of those lines have to be read as iambic pentameter, but to give them both the same rhythm would be a failure of sense. And so rhythm seems to take precedence over other kinds of pattern, including that of Williams' "variable foot."

  The critical problem of the variable foot is not eased or clarified by the example of traditional metrics, for in practice the iambic foot also is variable, and endlessly so. Once we have gone beyond the counting of syllables, there is no exact measure even of traditional line forms. Traditional scansion gives us a set number of syllables and, crudely, a set number of stresses, but it does not give us a reliable measure of pace or duration — as Pope demonstrated — or of emphasis. It can tell us roughly which or how many syllables to stress, but not how to weight the stresses with respect to sense. For example, in Warwick's speech on the death of the king in *Henry IV, Part II* —

> He's walked the way of nature,
> And to our purposes he lives no more.[1]

— much of the force and meaning will be determined by the emphasis given by the actor or reader to the word "our," but this emphasis cannot be determined from the meter. Or consider the following famous lines of blank verse:

> Of Mans First Disobedience, and the Fruit
> Of that Forbidden Tree, whose mortal taste
> Brought Death into the World, and all our woe . . .[2]

Are those lines of iambic pentameter, or ten-syllable lines each with four beats? And how much does this matter? I don't mean at all to suggest that it does not matter, but only that the question is a live one and ought to be asked. Could those lines be read with understanding and spoken intelligibly by a person who had never heard of blank verse or iambic pentameter? Of course they could. On the other hand, I am sure that as Milton composed those lines and the rest of *Paradise Lost*, he was continuously aware of the requirements of blank verse.

The Poetry of William Carlos Williams of Rutherford

Thus in reading (and also, I assume, in writing) even traditional verse, the issue of measure takes us quickly from the abstract metrical norm to such subjective standards as "understanding" or "sense of measure" or "sense of line" or "ear." Or we can say that if every actual line of poetry will inevitably vary from any abstract measure, then what properly should interest us is the intelligence or sensitivity of the variation. And maybe our only recourse in this difficulty is Pound's method of placing examples side by side and studying the differences, which also can be uncertain and difficult.

There is little point and no pleasure in reading Williams' poems or anybody else's as exemplifications of a theory of meter. We ought to keep aware, moreover, of the likelihood that metrical theories or schemes are more useful to poets than to readers. To a reader, a poem will be rhythmically coherent or not, and this can be understood without resort to scansion, whereas for a poet any metrical idea or standard that causes hesitation and revision is useful.

A poet gives a poem a rhythm peculiar to itself because of a sense that a poem must be made answerable to a standard external to itself. We apparently always have wanted and have felt we needed some sort of quantitative measure in poetry — as a sort of test perhaps, a way of making sure that it is done right. We recognize a rhythm by its regularity, and a poem, in its pauses and changes of sound, plays against the regularity of its rhythm. In his interview with *The Paris Review* (which displays cruelly his diminished ability to speak in the last year of his life), Williams says, "I wanted it to read regularly." And

Rhythm

again: "It's all in the ear. I wanted to be regular."[3] Without regularity there is no predictability, without predictability there can be no surprise, and without surprise there can be no "irrepressible freshness." But at last even surprise somehow must be accommodated formally.

Here again we come to the need to take care. Regularity, in the sense we are now likely to give to the term, is a mechanical regularity, that of a clock or metronome or engine. This sort of rhythm is a product of the industrial age; we could not have conceived of it before we had machines. Rhythms that I will call creaturely are radically different from mechanical rhythms, are less comprehensible and far more interesting.

This is a difference that seems to me indispensable to an understanding of poetry, and of much else, but I had not thought of it until, in 1997, I heard the British biologist Brian Goodwin speaking to a group of medical students on the subject of heart rhythm. A healthy heart, he said, does *not* beat with the invariable rhythm of a clock ticking. The heart, among all else that it is, is a *responsive* organ. Its beat must be approximately steady, but it also varies constantly and subtly in response to what is happening in the context of the body as a whole, as the body in turn responds to its constantly changing life within the contexts of place and events. And so every heartbeat, like every breath, is in a sense a unique creature, formed like our bodies, like our species, in response to events, conditions, and needs.

And so the idea of an invariable rhythm as the measure of a line or a poem is as false to poetry as the idea that a poem can be understood by extracting and paraphrasing its "meaning."

The Poetry of William Carlos Williams of Rutherford

The rhythm of a poem is creaturely, and for that reason it is significant. Though it is a work of art, a poem belongs to the creaturely world. The rhythms of the creaturely world are living, sensitive, responsive, and under influence. Everything in the creaturely world is under the influence of something else, and ultimately of everything else. Williams' poems belong, by his understanding and intention, to that world, and they resonate with it.

In reading a poem aloud, your sense of the regularity of its rhythm may be thrown a little off by your changing sense of what the poem is saying, or by your growing sense of its appropriateness to the circumstances in which it is being read. You can think of rhythm as a string on which beads are strung at intervals approximately regular. In Williams' satisfactory shorter poems, I believe the rhythm is likely to be continuous throughout, also taut so as to be under influence, and thus responsive; you get no response from a slack string. The rhythm, unlike scansion, continues through any longish pauses that may be required by sense or syntax, or by the endings of lines or stanzas. There will not be a sound for every beat, but I think that the natural stresses or emphases of what is being said will tend to fall on the beat.

Thoughts, memories, and emotions that exist simultaneously in the mind enter the sequence of literary composition by the help—the indispensable help, if the result is to have sense or value—of the ordering principle of rhythm. Chet Atkins once said (I believe I am remembering his language about right) that rhythm is nature's way of keeping everything from

Rhythm

happening at once. And it is by our sense of rhythm that we know we have the form right, that we have put everything in the right place at the right time.

ॐ

The Islamic scholar, Martin Lings, in writing about "the ritual dances of Sufism," said that "rhythm is a miraculous bridge between movement and repose, and amongst other things it is able to confer upon 'the dry bones of words' the power and privileges of music."[4] This seems to confirm again my assumption that rhythm is the fundamental musical principle of poetry.

It remains to be said that rhythm also involves a forward or onward movement. It sets the pace and has an energy, and these are formal limits. It is a weight-bearer of a certain strength, and so it can be under- or overloaded.

But rhythm is also a universal principle. It is the principle of coherence in our bodily functions, in most physical work, in work that is daily or seasonal, and so on. The rhythm of a poem, I suspect, is never without relation to rhythms external to it. Its rhythm may activate in the minds of poet and reader the sense or memory of those external rhythms and resonate with them. If poems mean more than they say, this is part of the reason. What distinguishes poetry, however, is not that it is rhythmic, but that its rhythms are segmented by the structures of lines. And so to the interaction or collaboration of two elemental members, line and sentence, we now have added a

The Poetry of William Carlos Williams of Rutherford

third: the poem's sustaining rhythm with which the other two also interact, by which they are influenced, and which they in turn influence.

We must consider also that the other musical means associated with poetry—the sound identities of rhyme, alliteration, assonance, and consonance—have the power of increasing stress and so of affecting rhythm. The second of a pair of rhyming words, for instance, is likely to be more heavily stressed and musically more significant than the first. These likenesses of sound certainly can be beautiful, but they are not necessarily ornamental. Rightly used, they belong intimately and organically to the poem and to what it is saying. Is there a difference between the poem and what it is saying? Williams certainly would have said no.

۔

ۀ **15** ۀ

The Structure
of Sounds

. . . .

  I have been talking for many pages about the art of poetry, which has mainly to do with the structure of the sounds a poem makes, as distinct from the structure of the sense it makes. But sense is necessarily always involved, for the structure of sound and the structure of sense, like the structures of lines and sentences, relate by collaboration and mutual influence, and can never be clearly divided. This art is enormously, even infinitely, complex. The forms just of lines and sentences are infinitely variable, and so must be their interactions.

  It is useful to ask how a line of poetry actually is measured, but it is useless to expect an answer that is simple or complete. I think the question is useful partly *because* it is so hard to answer. If we consider only that rhyme may become a part of rhythm, and rhythm a part of sense, then we see that no analysis, however fine, can produce a full description or explanation of the working of a poem, and it is good for us to know this.

To begin, the line to be measured has, or is, a length. Its length can be determined by sight, by the number of syllables or feet or stresses, and by its duration when spoken. If we are reading a poem aloud or hearing it read aloud—provided always that the poem be well made and well read—our sense of it as measured speech will be strongly affected, or perhaps determined, by our sense of the duration of each spoken line. Duration is the most critical issue, and the cause of the most trouble. The sense of duration is given by the way the reader presents the sound of a line both in itself and in relation to what precedes and follows it: its stresses and emphases, its rhythm, pace, and coherence or tensile strength, its pauses, and by the reader's sense of what it says. The arrangement of sounds and the sense of what is said will determine the length of a pause, or require a syllable to be dwelt on, as a singer may dwell on a note.

I don't think all this can be reduced to a scheme or a system of notation that would tell a reader precisely how to measure a line, or how to read it according to a measure precisely foreknown. It does not seem likely that poets or readers can be conscious as they write or read of all the concerns I have mentioned. But if they have dealt consciously with these concerns as they have read and thought about poetry, then such thoughts will inform their intuition and sensitivity as they write or read.

From all schemes and theories of measure and metrics, we are always going to be thrown back in a salutary and welcome defeat. When you are mindful of all that is involved in the making of a poem, schools of criticism and schools of composition, whatever their uses, will look small in the presence of poetry itself and of the good poems you know. The only equipment at all equal to those presences is the human mind, complete: imagination, intelligence, reason, instincts, senses, shared knowledge and loyalties, and the personal furniture of experience, memory, history, and culture. And insofar as that mind is conscious, it will be conscious of mysteries, of being baffled.

As human minds go, I think Williams had a good one. It was, as ought to be expected, unlike some other minds, as I am aware from my own failure at times to follow his thinking or to agree with him. But one indication of his intelligence was his ability to give throughout a poem the sense of rhythmic coherence and of measured speech, which is to say his poise. This is merely obvious in "The Dance," from *The Wedge* of 1944:

> In Brueghel's great picture, The Kermess,
> the dancers go round, they go round and
> around, the squeal and the blare and the
> tweedle of bagpipes, a bugle and fiddles
> tipping their bellies (round as the thick-
> sided glasses whose wash they impound)
> their hips and their bellies off balance
> to turn them. Kicking and rolling about
> the Fair Grounds, swinging their butts, those
> shanks must be sound to bear up under such

The Structure of Sounds

> rollicking measures, prance as they dance
> in Brueghel's great picture, the Kermess.[1]

This poem is well known, and for the best of reasons: it is lively as can be, a delight to read aloud or sound out in your mind. Scanning the lines will show you that the meter is irregular, highly variable, and yet the rhythm is regular, giving us steadily, from beginning to end and beyond, the beat of the imagined music. The lines, varying constantly, spiral round and round nevertheless in submission to the rhythm.

I will quote another poem, perhaps even more famous because so often liked and disliked. This poem, often called "The Red Wheel Barrow" though not titled by Williams when he published it in *Spring and All*, was written twenty or so years before "The Dance":

> so much depends
> upon
>
> a red wheel
> barrow
>
> glazed with rain
> water
>
> beside the white
> chickens [2]

The Poetry of William Carlos Williams of Rutherford

The pattern of stresses here is regular, the scansion of the lines irregular, and the rhythm, as in "The Dance," regular. It is a charming poem that presents a modest vision that is clear and life-affirming, beautiful in its way, if we consent to it. If we wish to understand Williams as a poet, it is important to notice that this poem's charm depends wholly upon its prosody. To write it out as a prose sentence would reduce it to a bland assertion followed by a mere list of things of little interest or consequence. But as Williams formed it on the page it both sings in the ear and lights up in imagination. Some readers may deal with this poem by asking, "So much *of what* depends upon . . . ?" Well, how seriously are we to take this little poem? Surely it is possible to like it very much without taking it *very* seriously. Are we to go about demanding to know *why* Peter the pumpkin eater could not keep his wife? I think Williams might reasonably have answered, "If you don't know, you can't be told." But don't we know that difficult and painful lives have been made livable by just such comely small visions as this poem gives us, and by somebody's ability to say such graceful things about them?

· III

The Structure of Sounds

A Love Poem

. . . .

Under the heading of measure and music, I could quote again "A Negro Woman," asking the reader to read it aloud more consciously than before as measured speech, and that would be a good thing to do. But here I will quote instead from the "Coda" of "Asphodel, that Greeny Flower," for in the following passage we are so clearly no longer listening to a middle-aged or aging poet urgently trying to achieve what he would consider a viable art of poetry; now we are listening to an old poet saying with all his art something he urgently needs to say to his wife:

> For our wedding, too,
>   the light was wakened
>   and shone. The light!
> the light stood before us
>   waiting!
>   I thought the world

stood still.
>At the altar
>>so intent was I
before my vows,
>so moved by your presence
>>a girl so pale
and ready to faint
>that I pitied
>>and wanted to protect you.
As I think of it now,
>after a lifetime,
>>it is as if
a sweet-scented flower
>were poised
>>and for me did open.[1]

Early in this book, after quoting "Young Woman at a Window," I said that Williams had learned to make of his own language a work that could be nothing but a poem. The passage I have just quoted fulfills that requirement exactly: It could be nothing but a poem. It says plainly what it means in language unquestionably fitting. Explanation or paraphrase would be pointlessly reductive. What it says could not be said with the same sense or to the same effect in prose. What it says it says in poetry, the singular speech, which alone, as Williams insisted, has the power to reveal us to ourselves, "as it makes / its transformations from the common / to the undisclosed and lays that open..."[2]

I don't think this passage calls upon us to linger over it in pondering and explaining. But we do linger over it in admiration, and we can usefully give some time to appreciating its remarkable quality. To see what Williams accomplished here, we can begin by noticing that "Asphodel, that Greeny Flower" is a love poem, and that I have quoted one of its most intimate passages. Love poetry presents a poet with a problem that is both peculiar and representative. It is peculiar because it is necessarily personal; an impersonal love poem simply is inconceivable. The problem is representative, characteristic of the art, because, like all subjects of poetry, it must be made more than personal—not public exactly, but communicable or recognizable to others. If a love poem, or any poem, is only personal, then it is insignificant and therefore absurd, like an exclamation on a T-shirt. It would be like reading a stranger's love letter, which at best would be uninteresting, at worst interesting for a wrong reason, as to a literary-industrial biographer. In a respectable love poem, the poet must speak not only to a beloved person but also for any reader. The poem must be authentically a work of art: something said, but also and just as necessarily something imagined and made. Otherwise the poem becomes an expression of incommunicable feeling, merely personal or self-expressive or sentimental. The poet, then, is obliged to speak not feelingly in words, as in a love letter, but in measure, in all senses of that phrase. In so speaking, the words are changed in sense from personal to imaginable. To Williams, imagination was the power of making real—of formally realizing, in its momentary presence, without the intervention of "ideas" or "fixed concepts," our actual experience.

At the time he was writing this poem, he was associating imagination with love and with light, trying again and again, out of a sense of difficulty perhaps, or even of ongoing failure, to articulate the connections among the three:

> But love and imagination
> are of a piece
> swift as the light
> to avoid destruction.[3]

And again: "Light, the imagination / and love / . . . maintain / all of a piece / their dominance."[4]

In the "Coda" before the passage on the poet's wedding, there is a building urgency, denoted by a momentum of speech under stress of measure. The poet, speaking characteristically as and for himself, has grown old, and he speaks with the knowledge that his time is running out. He has grown old in love and in marriage, a marriage that in certain respects he has failed. He has confessed his failure; he has received forgiveness. But he needs more than forgiveness. He needs to bring his life at last under the rule of love; he needs to believe that love is paramount and attains finally to a perfection ("Love without shadows"[5]) that is indestructible; he needs a vision. The formative image of this final meditation in the "Coda" is less a metaphor maybe than an analogy by which light, imagination, and love triumph over death and destruction:

Inseparable from the fire
       its light
              takes precedence over it.
Then follows
       what we have dreaded—
           but it can never
overcome what has gone before.
       In the huge gap
           between the flash
and the thunderstroke
       spring has come in
           or a deep snow fallen.
Call it old age.
       In that stretch
           we have lived to see
a colt kick up its heels.
       Do not hasten
           laugh and play
in an eternity
       the heat will not overtake the light.
       That's sure.
That gelds the bomb,
       permitting
           that the mind contain it.
This is that interval,
       that sweetest interval,
           when love will blossom,

A Love Poem

> come early, come late
> > and give itself to the lover.
> Only the imagination is real!

He prolongs his meditation, his "worship" of the triumphal light, which he first associates with imagination and love, and then with celebration, "medieval pageantry" and "the pomp and ceremony / of weddings," finally quoting from Spenser's "Prothalamion": "Sweet Thames, run softly / till I end / my song . . ." Under duress of need and the stress of an established measure of speech, the power of imagination gives him his vision:

> For our wedding, too,
> > the light was wakened
> > > and shone . . .[6]

The vision is a memory, but it is far more than that. By the means of his art the memory is restored to life and made present. But this presentation is *of* the imagination; it is not a description of the sort that we think of as "realistic." It is not a historical restoration or a "period piece." The sense of measure is formally powerful, excluding the nonessential and the merely realistic details, including only the details necessary to complete the rhythm and the sense. Thus the imagined sense is made: the memory is made "real," a vision presently experienced and fully known in the strange, unmodern immensity of a ceremony concluded by vows. He has entered again what at times he has thought of as an eternal moment; this time it is the moment of his marriage, whose sanctity he now recognizes as never before. It is a remarkable moment, not only in the life of this poet, but also in his poetry and in all the poetry I know. He can say that the flower was "poised / and for me did open," forsaking his concern for "the American idiom," because he sees now that his vows had joined him, as to his bride, also to Spenser and his great poetry of love and marriage.

What does this passage mean? I have so far avoided any direct dealing with the word "meaning" because, though I can't always avoid it, I don't much like it. "Meaning" belongs to the same family of words as "environment." It is a distancing word of abstraction and displacement, seeming always to refer to an idea that is separable and separate from any thing. If you say, "The poem means . . . ," you are about to say something in a language different from that of the poem, and also something similar to the "meaning" of any number of other poems.

In the passage at hand, as I think in all of Williams' poetry, there is no difference between what the lines say and what they mean. Their meaning is incarnate in what the poet has imagined and made, and what they say could have been said only in this poem.

෨෩

A Love Poem

The "Coda" is a celebration of light and is an act of faith. Does it matter that "the palm goes / always to the light"? It matters absolutely, for it is only in seeking and celebrating the light that we can come together, each of us out of our individual darkness, "the null / [that] defeats it all." [7] By such emissaries as the Negro woman with her luminous bouquet, bearing light "from another world," we are wakened and attracted. The imagination goes to them irresistibly and necessarily. In its truest manifestations the imagination draws the poet, and the rest of us, toward the light as we are drawn toward the opened windows of Matisse. This is Williams' generosity, his "gift outright," unhedged. And so even the "descent" of age, even defeat and despair, may bring us to "new places" where love may be perceived as shadowless, as light:

> Love without shadows stirs now
> > beginning to waken
> > > as night
> advances. [8]

The imagination may show us Hell, but not Hell alone. It shows us, beyond Hell, the beckoning light, to be reached even by descent. And thus the literature of unrelieved pain and horror is wrong. It is neither reality nor imagination but a strange nihilism of the modern mind that cherishes and dwells upon whatever is worst, "the death of all / that's past // all being" that Williams openly mocked:

But spring shall come and flowers will bloom
and man must chatter of his doom   .   .

And then follow the hard-earned stately measures:

The descent beckons
                as the ascent beckoned . . . 9

❧ 17 ❧

More on
the Context
of Locality

. . . .

A poem must be imagined in the process of its making. It must be made by art. It must be an artifact made of words. This making is what Williams seems to have meant by "invention." The bond between imagination and invention is indissoluble. They are two things, but one comes only with the other.

I began earlier a discussion of the difficulty Williams faced in doing his work, and now it is time to return to that subject and enlarge it, the better to understand his thoughts about imagination and invention. Actually he faced several difficulties, and, as I suggested before, all of them originate in his choice to live his life and do his work in Rutherford, New Jersey, where he was born. It is easy to think of Rutherford as a suburb of New

York City, for it is only a short distance away, "an easy commute." But Williams was not a commuter. He was intimately involved, by his daily life and work, in Rutherford and its surroundings. He was well-acquainted with the City and with certain people who lived there, but he could not easily go there, mainly, I think, because he could not spare the time. Though New York might be advertised, and with great force and influence, as the national center of the arts, Williams was centered, consciously and conscientiously, in Rutherford. His own art was centered there.

It was an American place, still culturally new and crude, long subjected to the continuously disruptive forces of industrial development, lacking the steadying and authenticating "peasant traditions" that its immigrant population had left behind. It was a place in want of a verifying or realizing imagination, of an adequate language, which is to say an adequate poetry.

From the perspective of New York and the cultural centers of Europe, it was a provincial place. Or, to be more precise, it was a place that an ambitious young poet could easily fear was provincial. From such places many writers of Williams' generation had fled in disdain or disgust to New York or London or Paris. He of course was well aware of this, and it seems to have troubled him. In a letter to Robert Lowell in 1952, he explained as follows his early and lasting resentment of T. S. Eliot: "But we were so weakly based, so uncertain of everything, that a mere breeze could capsize us—and did."[1] I don't know who he would have included in that "we" besides himself, but he certainly included himself. Eliot, as ambitious and for different reasons as uneasy as Williams, had clothed himself, so to speak, in the English cultural tradition, whereas Williams felt himself naked in New Jersey, confronting an unformed "mass of detail" and "the pure products of America [going] crazy."

Stubbornly but also courageously, and finally with results that entirely vindicated him, he made of his felt nakedness a working principle. In dealing with his place, his subject, he made himself naked to it by repudiating preconceived opinions about it. "No ideas but in things" is a poetic principle, but I think it is by implication a criticism of the European conquest of North America and its continuing history. We have lived in and exploited our country largely by preconception and wishful thinking, imposing on each new place we have come to the assumption that it is like the old place we have left, refusing to recognize where we are and to live within the limits of natural circumstance. The culminating and most egregious example of this is our refusal to this day to adapt ourselves to the aridity of the West, though we have come to terms with all parts of our country only occasionally and in spots. In our history, as Wallace Stegner among others has said, there has been a theme of settlement, adaptation, and caretaking. But though it has been persistent, that theme has been minor, always frustrated and often defeated by an economy of exploitation and the fashion of "getting somewhere" by going somewhere else. Williams, born in Rutherford, by some blessed intuition also awakened there to the need to know where he was, and to ask what might be required of him if he was to live and work there as usefully as he wished. And so he abandoned the handiness of "fixed

More on the Context of Locality

concepts" and refused to privilege ideas over things. Of course he did not abandon ideas, except as fetched-in abstractions that would have obscured or filtered his experience. He did not, for example, abandon the idea of love, but if there was to be love then it would be love for some person, place, or thing particularly known and imagined.

જ⃝

He was of course only human, caught like all of us within the limits of his mind and language. "No ideas but in things," thus stated, is an idea. But he was nonetheless right to reject the prevalent dissociation of ideas and things, mind and matter, and in doing so he was hardly unique among his contemporaries. Allen Tate, to name one, rejected what he called "the angelic imagination," which is divorced from the natural world, the senses, experience, and human scale. We will finally have to agree, I think, that the worthy ideas must be renewed again and again in things; they must materialize themselves; they must be made flesh. As Williams saw, as anybody who looks can now see, it is precisely in their granting of priority to ideas over things and over the world that the universities have failed us, for that priority is established and maintained by the industrial technology that oppresses and exploits the material world and all its bodies. We and our places and our world are free only when our minds accept the limits of a place and a local loyalty. Otherwise, "pure science" and "pure art" are put willy-nilly at the service of the industrial economy. The "cutting edge" of determining force is then embodied in workers who do not know what they are making, or obedient technicians in bombers or places of torture:

> as if the earth under our feet
> were
> an excrement of some sky
>
> and we degraded prisoners
> destined
> to hunger until we eat filth . . .[2]

He was right, but his principled renunciation exposed him directly to "a mass of detail / to interrelate on a new ground, difficultly . . ."[3]

A further difficulty was Williams' rejection of "presupposed measures"—the traditional verse forms—which he seems to have associated with "fixed concepts." I think it is a mistake to make an absolute of any technical proscription. But it is a fact, long thought upon by T. S. Eliot among others, that a way of writing can be used up. A technique, a way of making a line of verse, can "go dead." To get along without "presupposed measures," as he called them in *Spring and All*, was to commit himself to what later, in "Writer's Prologue to a Play in Verse," he called "composition, / without code."[4] He was doing his best to shove aside the clutter, the settled habits and prejudices of the made-up mind, that obtruded between himself and his neighbors and their actual circumstances and experience.

More on the Context of Locality

If we bear in mind Williams' pressing need for a language and a poetry adequate to the "mass of detail" that he faced daily in his chosen place, it is in no way surprising that he rejected the traditional prosody of English verse. He did so because the traditional forms of lines and stanzas stood obstructively between him and the experience he was trying to get at. Those forms seemed to him, reasonably, to call for experience and materials unlike or not at all his own. The adequate forms would have to be invented—a hardship that Williams conscientiously chose.

For this choice I have found no better justification than that provided by Czeslaw Milosz's "Quarrel with Classicism" in *The Witness of Poetry*. Milosz's terms and his occasion are somewhat different from Williams', but the following passage pertains uncannily to Williams' predicament in Rutherford:

> In his famous work *Mimesis* Erich Auerbach pointed to a certain lack of reality wherever a convention is used: where the poet creates as beautiful a structure as possible out of topoi universally known and fixed, instead of trying to name what is real and yet unnamed. Thus the literary conventions which bind author and reader form a barrier, and it is difficult to step beyond it into chaotic reality with its inexhaustible richness of detail.[5]

Milosz says further that since the beginning of the modern era, which he puts in the sixteenth century, poets have tended to visualize an order located somewhere else, in a different place or time. Such longing, by its nature eschatological, is directed against every "here and now . . ." [6]

Form, in Williams' sense of it, is not a vessel to be filled, such as a bowl or an Italian sonnet. Instead, form and content grow together, are "fleshed out" in the course of happening, like a hand or a tree. His antipathy to ready-made forms or "presupposed measures" in poetry is justified by the analogies between such forms and all preconceived or conventional forms that are *imposed* upon experience or upon the world.

Milosz's understanding of artistic convention as a sort of oblivion converges with Robert Duncan's understanding of conventional form as control. Duncan found a telling analogy for this in the "military arts": "Men are drilled in order that there be an authority, removing them from immediate concern in the acts of killing and destruction involved." [7] This returns us, by further analogy, to the rational or geometric formality, with consequent disorder and damage, imposed on the earth by explosives and machinery: the building of dams and levees, stream-straightening, the anti-topographic geometries of industrial agriculture, all forms of surface mining. The American "new world" opened to us like a flower, to be defaced, desecrated, and plundered—this thought afflicted Williams all his life.

After these just and proper blamings of convention, however,

More on the Context of Locality

it is necessary to say that, to the extent that art and human life are artificial, are not natural but *made*, a certain amount of convention has to be accommodated. A poem, after all, is made of language, a medium never entirely satisfactory, but to be usable at all a language has to remain conventional to a considerable degree among its users. We have to agree on the sounds of letters, the senses of words, and the general patterns of sentence structure.

There may be also a sense of form as fidelity that applies to Williams' work. This is form as "sticking with it," awaiting what may be revealed. In this sense, Williams' commitment to life and practice in his "province" is formative and a kind of form. It is a form, I think, analogous to marriage, a conventional form that is opposite, as both the vows and Williams' late love poems suggest, to form-as-preconception.

☙

By his choice of a place and by his rejection of conventional means of dealing with it, Williams was a man in difficulty—a man, as it must have seemed to him, in a perplexity of difficulties. Why should we blame him, then, for his attempts through much of his life to develop theories, which were attempts to rationalize his intuitions or his practice, or to tell himself what he was trying to do? You can follow this effort through *The Collected Poems*, of which the art of poetry is a persistent concern, working your way from one of its manifestations to another, making connections and continuities of sense as well as you can. But I think you will be misled in doing so if you suppose that, behind it all, there is a complete *ars poetica*. For Williams was working all his life *toward* an ars poetica, not *from* one. For myself, I like this incompleteness, because I don't believe that a theory of art, as opposed to works of art, can be complete.

Allen Tate said, in reference to Williams' "dogma" of the misfit between American speech and iambic poetry, "It seems that Williams needed bad theories to write good poetry." [8] That is a neat thing to say and I willingly enjoy it, but I would count it only partly true. Williams did write good poetry, but not all of his theories were bad. I have made clear my distrust of "the variable foot." And I am sure that "the American idiom" was not singular and that it never existed anywhere as such; Williams' local idiom was different from Faulkner's, and both are different from mine. But Williams' writing over forty years (at least) about imagination and invention, so far as I have been able to understand it, is substantive and useful.

More on the Context of Locality

18

The Prose
of *Spring*
and All

. . . .

My intention throughout this book has been to concentrate as exclusively as possible on the texts of *The Collected Poems* and *Paterson*, referring to Williams' prose books only as necessary. But my task is both helped and complicated by the presence of some prose in the two volumes of poetry, and particularly by the prose passages inserted among the poems of *Spring and All*, published in 1923. My attention to these passages brings me into confrontation with critics who have thought them to be little better than nonsense. Because we are imperfect humans, something usually must be conceded to detraction, and so for anybody's impatience with the prose in *Spring and All* I have to acknowledge that there are reasons.

Spring and All, especially in the devices and manners of the prose, involves a good bit of horsing around. At certain points early in the sequence, chapter headings are inserted, though they could as well be done without, and these are numbered inconsecutively with both Arabic and Roman numerals. For instance, "Chapter XIII" comes second, after "Chapter 19," and the former heading is printed upside down. The paragraphs are divided by double spaces, inclining them toward more independence than paragraphs usually have, and hinting that they are less sequential than they sometimes are. There are what appear to be "notes" put down in a hurry. There are sentences that don't end, that don't begin, that are strung together with dashes. There is some hyperbole and bluster.

This levity may be accounted for in several ways. The prose passages were not included in *The Collected Earlier Poems* of 1951, in which I first read the poems of *Spring and All*. When I came upon the original edition in the late '50s, though I read the prose with much interest, I saw the oddities I have mentioned as amusing "experimentation" or "modernism." Maybe I was to some extent right, and I still think them amusing. But now I suspect that Williams was deliberately pulling the noses of Very Serious Critics who would offer their noses to be pulled. The outrage of some obliging critics makes me think that I am right.

Without discarding my first two explanations, after long pondering I want to add a third. I think that when Williams wrote the prose of *Spring and All* he was dealing with issues of the greatest and most immediate importance both to his work and to his understanding of its cultural importance. Like Eliot and Pound, he was never working just for the success of poetry, but also for the success of culture in the broadest sense. But Eliot and Pound were working for a culture that ultimately was cosmopolitan and construed from the top down, whereas Williams, more "difficultly," was working from the bottom up for a culture that was not only American but also local. He was confronting issues about which he was urgently serious while at the same time he was unconfident and troubled about his ability to deal with them. He needed a mask of unseriousness, so to speak, in order to be serious.

Well into this work he speaks openly of his difficulty:

> I think often of my earlier work and what it has cost me not to have been clear. I acknowledge I have moved chaotically about refusing or rejecting most things, seldom accepting values or acknowledging anything.

Here he is referring to his rejection of "fixed concepts" and "presupposed measures," and he is far from either horseplay or confusion. He then proceeds to a definition of his problem:

> I early recognized the futility of acquisitive understanding and at the same time rejected religious dogmatism. My whole life has been spent (so far) in seeking to place a value upon experience and the objects of experience that would satisfy my sense of inclusiveness without redundancy . . .
>
> But though I have felt "free" only in the presence of

· 135

The Prose of Spring and All

works of the imagination, knowing the quickening of the sense which came of it, and though this experience has held me firm at such times, yet being of a slow but accurate understanding, I have not always been able to complete the intellectual steps which would make me firm in the position.[1]

As I generally am going to do in dealing with these passages, I have quoted only what is clear to me. Not all the language of these paragraphs is clear to me—not all of it may have been clear to Williams; as I have said, he was in difficulty—but what I understand I admire and am grateful for. The imaginative means of placing a proper value upon experience and the objects of experience, the freedom bestowed by works of imagination—these are subjects of momentous interest to any serious poet or reader. Williams' confession of his inability to complete the intellectual steps that would gather these subjects into a clearly comprehensible theory was put down by Donald Davie as the boastful self-revelation of "a muddlehead." But I think that Williams in fact went a long way toward a complete theory of imagination and art, and that his theory, as far as he took it, is authentic. As for his confession, I can only add my own, which is the same as his, and with the comfort only of my doubt that anybody can put in place all the intellectual steps.

19

The Eternal
Moment and
the Ground
Underfoot

. . . .

Now I want to return to the early pages of *Spring and
All* and go through to the end, speaking of the passages that
give most light and clarity to my understanding of Williams'
concerns. Before doing that, however, I need to acknowledge
the ease of my task in comparison to his. I have the benefit of
hindsight from the rest of Williams' work. He, by contrast,
was beating a track through a thicket that no poet had entered
before: his own experience in his own place and its continuously accumulating detail. This he had to contend with in order
to be true to himself, and he had to make a poetry capable of

contending with it in order to be true to the power and promise of his art.

He begins by speaking of "the reader," and by this phrase he apparently means all of us, himself included, who have the problem that he wishes to address:

> There is a constant barrier between the reader and his consciousness of immediate contact with the world . . . [T]he thing he never knows and never dares to know is what he is at the moment that he is. And this moment is the only thing in which I am at all interested.

Ignoring for the moment the examples he is going to adduce in his support, he says that "nearly all writing . . . if not all art, has been especially designed to keep up the barrier . . ." And then he sets forth what I take to be his first principle:

> To refine, to clarify, to intensify that eternal moment in which we alone live there is but a single force—the imagination.[1]

Though Williams did not develop his work in reference to a church or sect, he was by no means a materialist. He was a true poet, accepting all the language he could bring into use, and when the need for them arose he did not back away from such words as "eternal," "worship," "holiness," "grace," "sacred," and "faith." His understanding of imagination he brings to rest upon the assumption that we are eternal creatures, living only in the "eternal moment," to which only imagination can awaken us. Awake in that moment, we would not only be vitally alive, as usually we are not, but also would be able to make valid choices about how to live, rather than submitting passively to our commercial degradation.

For the sake of this awakening, the imagination must be "freed from the handcuffs of 'art,'" by which he means art dulled by a trite formality. Our life, revealed by imagination so freed, is a new world, a springtime world, where "HOPE long asleep [is] aroused once more."[2]

Imagination, properly functioning, may reveal to the artist both present circumstances and the work that must be done. This is exemplified by the third poem of *Spring and All*:

> The farmer in deep thought
> is pacing through the rain
> among his blank fields, with
> hands in pockets,
> in his head
> the harvest already planted.
> A cold wind ruffles the water
> among the browned weeds.
> On all sides
> the world rolls coldly away:
> black orchards
> darkened by the March clouds—
> leaving room for thought.
> Down past the brushwood

The Eternal Moment and the Ground Underfoot

bristling by
the rainsluiced wagonroad
looms the artist figure of
the farmer—composing
—antagonist [3]

Not only is this a fine poem, but—for a rarity—it grants to the farmer his true worth and dignity. The farmer is seen properly as an "artist figure." He is seen, moreover, as walking between two worlds: the world of reality perceived (and by imagination made real) as it immediately is, and the world of an imagined futurity in which the work of "composing" must be done. What the farmer is composing is his work of the growing season, "the harvest already planted" in his mind. In him "there is the residual contact between life and the imagination which is essential to freedom."[4]

I admire the poem and see no problem in it. But it complicates the theoretical issues with which Williams is struggling. The farmer is seen as an "antagonist," maybe, because the "contact" between life or reality and imagination is—in reality—hard if not impossible to make clear. Also, insofar as he is "composing," he is antagonistic to disorder. The poem represents an eternal moment in which the poet is clearly and intensely aware of what he is seeing. While he is composing his poem he is living in that moment. But the farmer is living in two such moments: the present one in which he is bound to be aware of the same winter scene with himself in it that the poet is aware of, but also a present vision of the future crop year—as the poet's later remembering of his wedding becomes a present vision of the past. In every instance, we are talking about a moment that is present, whether it involves past, present, or future. The problem might be more easily resolved if we could think of the farmer as "lost" in his composing, but he is composing in and with respect to a place that requires attention, not on a blank canvas or page. If in fact he is in an eternal moment in which he is composing a relationship between what presently is and what is yet to come, both sides of the relationship come under the rule of imagination; and then where is the point of "contact between life and the imagination" and what is the nature of that contact? Our task of understanding becomes yet more difficult when we consider that the reader, who is absorbed in the eternal moments of the poet and the farmer, is presumably living in a moment of his own in which he is experiencing the eternal moment of the poem, which presumably will clarify for him the eternal moment of his own contact with the world.

I have just written out a sort of riddle for which I doubt that there is an answer. We have a series of relationships—of the poet with his poem, of the farmer with his still-wintery farm and his composition of the coming year, of the reader with the poem and his own circumstances. None of those relationships is in itself confusing. But we are dealing with relationships of relationships, and the function of the key term, "imagination," apparently shifts as we move from one relationship to another. A further problem is that the realization of the eternal moment, for farmer or poet or reader or any of us humans, is at best

The Eternal Moment and the Ground Underfoot

fleeting. The riddle ultimately may be that of time and eternity. How do we live in either or in both, and what is their relationship?

It is, in any event, lovely and enriching to see that the poem of the farmer appears to involve three eternal moments—the farmer's, the poet's, the reader's—like three windows aligned.

I believe, like Williams, in the eternal moment, partly because I believe that eternity is as much a condition of reality as is time, partly because I don't believe that the temporal duration of the present moment is measureable. I also believe that there is a "contact between life and imagination" that is not only "essential to freedom," but is indispensable to human life.

It is imagination, surely, that is the source of the "irrepressible freshness" that Pound sought in works of art. By imagination we discover "the secret of that form // interknit with the unfathomable ground / where we walk daily . . ."[5] By imagination even the descent into old age, even defeat, "opens" a world, "a place / formerly / unsuspected," and so is "a reversal / of despair."[6] The "greater" world of imagination enlivens our sense of the world "we share with the / rose in bloom," so that the rose's scent may "startle us anew."[7] It is ever opposed to "the null / [that] defeats it all."[8] The imagination, then, is a superior kind of knowledge, the only sort of knowledge available to us that is formally complete. It has the power of making real to us the ordinary drama of our daily lives. The two poles of Williams' imagination were the eternal moment and the ground underfoot. The imaginative possibilities of an unfamiliar place are quickly used up. A "travel writer" has to keep moving. But with familiarity a place becomes to the imagination inexhaustible. This understanding was a principal motive of Williams' poetry for many years. If we follow it as a sort of theme through *The Collected Poems*, then we may readily assent to his affirmation in "Asphodel, That Greeny Flower" that "Only the imagination is real!"

But Williams insisted so fervently upon his principle of the reality of the imagination that we need to give some thought to it. The problem is that, in common usage, "imagination" is often opposed to any sense of reality, as when we say, "You are imagining things," meaning that the things you imagine do not exist. But we must remember that to Coleridge and Blake, among others, to imagine was to see things in their most real or eternal aspect. We may read "only the imagination is real" as "only what we have imagined is real to us," which is right enough. But by "imagination" I think Williams means also a mental faculty or realm in which, *only* in which, the reality of the real is fully recognized. Imagination is the power to see things in their "eternal moment" in which, *only* in which, they are real and we are alive. It is this, the convergence of the eternal and the present, that is possible and that is real only in imagination.

Poetry, then, is the means of giving to realizations of the fleeting eternal moment a kind of permanent presence, so that amid the confusions of the ever-accumulating mass of details they can be returned to, not as ends in themselves, I assume, but as reminders of an indispensable possibility, a wakefulness, belonging to the highest definition of our humanity.

Only the imagination is real also because it is in a sense one of our limits. We can live in a place only as we have imagined it with a sort of fidelity to itself, or as we have failed to do so. It is possible, as we have proved, to live and die "miserably" in the true desert of our failure, like bad farmers, to imagine the ground under our feet either as it is or as it might become— a failure that is making of our country a ruin in fact. It is this failure that accounts for the urgency with which Williams invariably addresses our need for poetry as a language of imagination. "Would it disturb you," he asks the audience in "Writer's Prologue to a Play in Verse," "if I said / you have no other speech than poetry?" Poetry, he tells them, is "the undiscovered / language of yourself" and "it can make transformations." He asks them to believe that poetry will

> re-dress
> itself humbly in that which you
> yourself will say is the truth, the
> exceptional truth of ordinary people . . . [9]

This is another of the poems in which Williams is speaking directly to his neighbors, seeking to instruct them and to make their lives better. If, as Hugh Kenner wrote, this was "Rutherford, where no one was listening," what are we to make of that? "In Rutherford," Kenner thought, Williams "might as well have lived in Paris." [10] This assumes, in the way of "universal" or "global" modernism, that the poetry came from nowhere, or that it could have or might as well have. It assumes also that

Williams lived, like other moderns, in a general condition of no neighbors and no audience, and it does so by brushing aside the fact that Williams' poems came from Rutherford and that his audience of first choice were his neighbors, to whom he sometimes spoke directly in his poems, regardless of whether or not they were listening. The right question is not whether they were listening then, but whether they (and we) should be listening now.

The point at issue is that Williams apparently did not see poetry as a part of high culture forever above ordinary life, or, like Pound, as a high perch from which to harangue the general multitude. Williams is speaking instead as a plain citizen who sees poetry as one of a set of vital concerns—along with medicine, economy, science, politics, education, etc.—that ought to be heard speaking locally together. That they should so speak and be so heard was a matter of greatest importance. As a part of the necessary conversation of a local culture, poetry becomes more urgently important than it can ever be as a high-cultural or academic specialty.

Years later we find the same sense of urgency in "Asphodel, That Greeny Flower":

> Look at
> what passes for the new.
> You will not find it there but in
> despised poems.
> It is difficult
> to get the news from poems

The Eternal Moment and the Ground Underfoot

> yet men die miserably every day
> > for lack
> of what is found there.[11]

Williams is talking about poems as cultural properties that have the power to keep us in touch with the ground under our feet. He seems to have kept for much of his life the conviction that in poetry we can say things that could not otherwise be said:

> Be patient that I address you in a poem,
> > there is no other
> > > fit medium.
> The mind
> > lives there. It is uncertain,
> > > can trick us and leave us
> agonized. But for resources
> > what can equal it?
> > > There is nothing.[12]

Williams goes on, in the prose of *Spring and All*, to assure us that there is nothing in his book that is not understood as "of a piece" with local nature, and that "Composition is in no essential an escape from life." His work, he says, will avoid "crude symbolism," "strained [literary] associations," and "complicated ritualistic forms designed to separate the work from 'reality'...."[13] The poems, in short, will take their value, not from subjects that they contain or refer to, but instead from their artistry and the power of imagination that is in them.

The above rejection of symbolism, associations, and ritualistic forms has to do, I assume, with Williams' antipathy to T. S. Eliot, but Eliot would certainly have agreed that the quality of a poem is not granted to it by its contents. Williams nevertheless is being true to himself and his work in struggling to articulate a connection between composition and life or imagination and reality. In reading through his poems, you feel him working unrestingly back and forth between the natural fact and the artifact, urged always toward the artifact and the imagination, and yet always affectionate toward the facts, the massed details as he saw them, and reluctant to give them up to art. Sometimes he surrenders to the attraction of a "finished" work of art. Sometimes he forcibly extends the radius of his art into the world of facts, cramming more and yet more of that world into a poem, as if the poem were a captive goose being stuffed for foie gras. He never resolved, probably he never wanted to resolve, the tension between facts or "events" and "language which they / forever surpass."[14]

This tension, this alternation of apparently contradictory impulses, belongs to the conversation between the poet and his place. As a poet, and also as a local citizen, he wishes to include all his world in his art, and thus to bring it under the rule and into the dignity, the usefulness, the truth and beauty, of imagination. But the place does not exist to be made into art, but has an independent existence of its own. Sometimes by the power of art the place can be persuaded, within limits, within measure, to submit to imagination; sometimes it resists. We do not necessarily contradict Blake, who thought the arts were

The Eternal Moment and the Ground Underfoot

our way of conversing with Paradise, if we say that they can also be our way of conversing with our earthly places. Blake picked up one end of that string, Williams the other. It is most important, I think, to see that the two ends belong to the same string. What we know of Paradise we learn here, by looking, by vision, by imagination, and both Paradise and the ground underfoot are always beyond the perfect grasp of our arts, as of our sciences.

The Poetry of William Carlos Williams of Rutherford

❧ **20** ❧

Completeness

. . . .

Only the imagination can give us knowledge that is formally complete. What Williams has to say in *Spring and All* about the completing power of imagination is of pressing importance to us as poets and readers, citizens and neighbors.

He begins his argument by addressing the issue of limits, specifically the "humiliation" of our smallness in proportion to all that the universe sets before us to know or experience or consume:

> Even the most robust constitution has its limits, though the Roman feast with its reliance upon regurgitation to prolong it shows an active ingenuity, yet the powers of man are so pitifully small, with the ocean to swallow— that at the end of the feast nothing would be left but suicide.[1]

Perhaps our natural response to abundance is gluttony or greed, which Williams rejects both because our capacity is humiliatingly small and because the desire itself to be all-consuming is suicidal. That this is an issue at once cultural and economic is clearly implied by Williams' language and his metaphor, and the gravity of the issue has increased distressingly in the eighty-seven years since the publication of *Spring and All*. For in that time those who adhere to greed as the proper motive and mode of life have established all-consumption as the paramount economic doctrine: unlimited economic growth. People opposed to this "ideology of the cancer cell," as Edward Abbey called it, will invoke against it the fact of ecological limits. The conservationist will argue that by studying the limits of ecosystems (which we are unlikely ever to understand completely) we will "figure out" how much we can consume. Without denying the importance or even the necessity of such study, I think Williams' solution is the correct one, and it comes from art, not from science or mathematics.

That limitless consumption is impossible does not make the desire for it less destructive. As an antidote Williams proposes simply the possibility of completeness or fullness:

> The stomach is full, the ocean no fuller, both have the same quality of fullness. In that, then, one is equal to the other. Having eaten, the man has released his mind.[2]

Of all the prose statements of *Spring and All*, this is the one that seemed richest to me when I first read it, and it has stayed with me through the years. It places exactly the point at which culture must depart from nature if we are to preserve either. Imagination and its works give us the possibility of completeness short of totality or infinity. If we are complete, then we don't have to be limitlessly greedy — and forever disappointed. We don't have to consume the whole creation or burst. And so the value of art is not in illusion to distract us from the bitterness of life. On the contrary,

it rouses rather than stupefies the intelligence by demonstrating the importance of personality, by showing the individual, depressed before it, that his life is valuable — when completed by the imagination.[3]

So completed, "having eaten," the mind is set free, to a necessary extent, from the world. And Williams later adds the obvious corollary: that by our imaginative completion of ourselves, the world, to a necessary extent, is set free from us. No longer needing to see it as "ours," we see it as a creature existing in its own integrity, in its own right, freely, as itself:

The writer of imagination would find himself released from observing things for the purpose of writing them down later. He would be there to enjoy, to taste, to engage the free world, not a world which he carries like a bag of food, always fearful lest he drop something or someone get more than he.

A world detached from the necessity of recording it
    . . .[4]

By such completions both the poet and the reader may see
that, as the world's parts or belongings, we must live in it on
its terms, not ours.

❧ **21** ❧

Imagination, Invention, and Reality

. . . .

From the requirement of imaginative completeness, it follows that a work of art must not be an illusion of reality. The artist must not "plagiarize" from nature. To do so—to paint as an illusion of "reality" a scene or a view—is to make a thing that is by nature fragmentary; both artist and viewer must accept thereby a sort of condemnation to incompleteness. In opposition Williams describes a painting, "The Open Window," by Juan Gris:

> Here is a shutter, a bunch of grapes, a sheet of music, a picture of sea and mountains . . . which the onlooker is not for a moment permitted to witness as an "illusion."[1]

Or, to use another example that Williams also seems to have had in mind, a landscape by Cézanne looks, as it should, forthrightly like a painting, not like an opened window. A work by Cézanne or Gris "escapes plagiarism after nature and becomes a creation"[2] — that is to say it becomes a creature in addition to the other creatures — with the power to "stand between man and nature as saints once stood between man and the sky . . ."[3]

Williams thus was in rebellion against the notion that the function of imagination is to "make up" clever deceptions or real-seeming illusions to serve us as "escapes" from the difficult truths of our lives. He rejects as copying or plagiarism Hamlet's proposition that art is a mirror held up to nature, and proposes instead that art is an imitation of the processes or creativity of nature. In this he places himself within a lineage that is honorable and old. In the traditional view going back to Plato, according to Amanda Coomaraswamy, "Art is an imitation of the nature of things, not of their appearances."[4] This seems to be the precedent that Coleridge had in mind when he wrote in *Biographia Literaria*:

> The primary IMAGINATION I hold to be the living Power and prime Agent of all human Perception, and as a repetition in the finite mind of the eternal act of creation in the infinite I AM.[5]

Reference to the I AM of Exodus would not come so readily to Williams, but his thought is nonetheless conformable to Coleridge's. Nor is it much at odds with Blake, who did not

The Poetry of William Carlos Williams of Rutherford

want painting reduced to "the sordid drudgery of fac-simile representations of merely mortal and perishing substances ..."[6] Maybe most useful of all is the following brief paragraph from Karl Ernst Osthaus's account of his visit to Cézanne in 1906. Cézanne had remarked that Courbet was "As great as Michelangelo" except that "he lacks 'elevation.'" Osthaus then comments:

> These remarks magnificently completed his lesson on his own painting. They proved that the supreme law of all art was known and familiar to him: without "elevation" beyond the surface appearance of things, without grasping the eternal in nature, there was for him, in the end, no art.[7]

Williams was passionately interested in the arts, in the powers of imagination, in the making of poetry. But as always in his thinking, his interest in these things was never "just aesthetic" or "just artistic." He was interested in the power of art to *place* us imaginatively, and therefore effectively, in our lives and in our local whereabouts. And so his concerns about art always have a dimension that is practical and ethical. Art is different from nature and, because contained within it, is subordinate to it. It must not plagiarize nature or trade in "lifelike" illusions, because it must not usurp the rule of nature either in the world or in the mind. We cannot live, let alone make an art or a culture, in an illusion of reality or a copy or a reflection of nature.

Imagination, Invention, and Reality

I take pleasure in noticing here that Williams' understanding of the relation of art to nature conforms exactly to the fundamental principle of the agricultural scientists Sir Albert Howard and Wes Jackson. Farming obviously cannot copy nature because it is to a significant extent an art and is to that extent artificial; it uses plants and animals that have been to some extent domesticated, and are to the same extent unnatural. But farming, according to Howard and Jackson, must nevertheless imitate the creativity of nature by incorporating the natural principles and processes of the forest or the prairie. The good farmer farms, then, not by a "realistic" copying, but by a kind of science, a kind of art, and a kind of imagination.

To copy nature may require great skill but, in Williams' terms, an inferior art. To imitate the creativity of nature, on the contrary, requires the art of a maker or creator who makes, not a mirror image, but a new creature. And this requires always, and in the highest sense, the use of imagination. "The imagination," Williams said, "is an actual force comparable to electricity or steam . . ." [8] To me, that seems misstated, a stroke of hyperbole that Williams in his mood of idol-breaking could not resist. I agree that the imagination is an actual force, but I would make it comparable in force to the force of rational thought or emotion or memory.

☙❧

The Poetry of William Carlos Williams of Rutherford

Now, having dealt with the relation of imagination to "the eternal moment" and to reality, I must return to the question of imagination and what Williams speaks of as "invention." The two terms may be conceptually or functionally inseparable, but Williams uses both and apparently felt that he needed both. He appears to use them not quite as synonyms.

In about the middle of *Spring and All*, the word "imagination" begins to have a more practical or technical implication than it has had before:

The value of the imagination to the writer consists in its ability to make words. Its unique power is to give created forms reality, actual existence. [9]

Earlier, "imagination" had the sense of vision, realization, authentic knowledge, perhaps of what, later, he would call "light." Here it has the sense of "art," as a way of making. The imagined thing must become a made thing. It must at last *be* a made thing. But it becomes an imagined thing to its maker also in the process of its making. From this comes Williams' unending preoccupation with the technique of verse. It is this aspect or function of imagination that he comes to name "invention." Invention apparently is the technical means of imagination, uniting vision or inspiration with the right words in the right order, divided or measured rightly into lines of verse:

Imagination, Invention, and Reality

· ·

the small foot-prints
of the mice under the overhanging
tufts of the bunch-grass will not
appear: without invention the line
will never again take on its ancient
divisions when the word, a supple word,
lived in it . . .[10]

That is from Book Two of *Paterson*. In *Spring and All*, he says
that "poetry has to do with the dynamization of emotion into a
separate form . . . . a new form dealt with as a reality in itself." [11]
He is still unfinished with this thought when he writes in his
introduction to *The Wedge* of 1944 that "There is no poetry
of distinction without formal invention."[12] It is by invention,
I suppose, that the poet negotiates "The jump between the
fact and the imaginative reality"[13] — though that quotation is a
sentence fragment that seems to float alone amid the prose of
Spring and All. But a few pages later he returns, as the first step
of a sort of recapitulation, to the issue of fact:

> The inundation of the intelligence by masses of com-
> plicated fact is not knowledge.
>
> It is the imagination on which reality rides . . .

It is for this reason that I have always placed art first and esteemed it over science . . .

Art is the pure effect of the force upon which science depends for its reality—Poetry

The effect of this realization upon life will be the emplacement of knowledge in a living current . . .[14]

Williams, then, saw art, realized imagination, as a force that kept knowledge from becoming inert. Knowledge emplaced by art, by imagination-as-vision and imagination-as-invention, in the current of lived life cannot be reduced either to mere facts or to fixed concepts.

∞

By the time of "Deep Religious Faith" in *The Desert Music*, "invention" seems to have meant to Williams the whole complex of powers required to do and to make—in short, to live. By then he had endured serious strokes and debilitating depression. How to continue had become a question of means, no longer only of poetry, but also of living. Religious faith therefore is not, or must not be, passive or merely "spiritual." It is a motivating force to "drive" us "Past death / past rainy days," and "beyond the remote borders / of poetry itself . . ." Perhaps this faith is the liveliness of life itself, comprehending poetry,

Imagination, Invention, and Reality

which poetry must strive to imitate. It gave us the saints of El
Greco, but it has humbler results just as important:

> It is what in life drives us
> to praise music
> and the old
> or sit by a friend
> in his last hours.

> All that which makes the pear ripen
> or the poet's line
> come true!
> Invention is the heart of it.

> Without the quirks
> and oddnesses of invention
> the paralytic is confirmed
> in his paralysis . . .

The poem concludes—surprisingly, perhaps, for a doctor
trained in medical science; unsurprisingly for a doctor who is
also a poet, who has "always placed art first and esteemed it
over science"—with an indictment of materialist poets:

> Shame on our poets,
> they have caught the prevalent fever:
> impressed
> by the "laboratory,"

                    they have forgot
                            the flower!
                                    which goes beyond all
            laboratories!
                    They have quit the job
                            of invention.[15]

   The prose of *Spring and All* goes on to a discussion of the
difference between prose and verse, which I confess I have
not understood. The twenty-sixth poem of the series perhaps
recalls the "eternal moment" by the mere mention of "beauty
/ the eternal." But I have said what I am able to say of the argument or manifesto of that book, and have made as much sense
of it as I am able to make by the dubious method of dealing with
the parts I understand and ignoring the rest. But the sense I
have made seems to me to be Williams' sense, not mine, though
it is confirming and encouraging to me. If it is my sense, then I
protest that I could not have made it except by pondering over
Spring and All.

   From the poem "Writer's Prologue to a Play in Verse" I get
the further suggestion that "meaning," to Williams, was simply
what is recognized in a poem as true. I don't think he believed
that meaning is something remote or mute or "hidden" in the
language of a poem that has to be probed out by analysis or
explanation. From the later poems, it is plain that he associated
the imagination with light, love, beauty, and truth, but how this
association might be spelled out is not clear. With such issues,
and probably with all issues related to the making and meaning

Imagination, Invention, and Reality

of art, we are humbled and eventually silenced by the difficulty mentioned earlier: that of discussing in sequence processes that occur simultaneously and even instantaneously.

And so, having acknowledged the incompleteness of this effort of mine, I am going to allow it to be reabsorbed into my long-standing love for Williams' poetry, and pass on to other matters I have saved for last.

❧ **22** ❧

Williams
and Eliot

. . . .

Williams' poems are not meant to plagiarize reality. Though they insist upon containing "the anti-poetic," they do not fall into the conventional trap of the "realism" that recognizes reality only by the violence, selfishness, and despair of the individualistic modern individual, alone for want of an adequate language. Nor do they imitate modern American disorder—though they willingly risk disorder. They attempt poetic form and cultural order in the names of imagination, beauty, and love. In his wish for a distinctly American poetry in "the American idiom," Williams was theoretically if always critically a nationalist, but his practice, of poetry as of medicine, was local. As a poet he attempted a practicable local patriotism— if that word by now signifies anything at all.

His local orientation and commitment is the basis of Williams' resentment of T. S. Eliot, which was bitter and long. As

Williams understood it, the trouble began with the publication of *The Waste Land*, which was "the great catastrophe to our letters" just because it was a distraction:

> There was heat in us [that is, in Williams and his American allies], a core and a drive that was gathering headway upon the theme of a rediscovery of a primary impetus, the elementary principle of all art, in the local conditions. Our work staggered to a halt for a moment under the blast of Eliot's genius which gave the poem back to the academics. We did not know how to answer him.[1]

It is easy to sympathize with Williams in this. The publication of *The Waste Land* was an international literary event of enormous impact and celebrity. It must have seemed to make light of the work of an uncelebrated local poet trying to make a poetry fit for Rutherford, New Jersey. And it did give academics a new hold on poetry. The academic industry of literary explanation gained new life and stature by feasting upon *The Waste Land*, thus helping to define poetry-reading as work for specialists and to propagate among nonspecialists the customary belief that they "can't understand poetry." This is a disaster, but I don't think it is an outcome that Eliot could have intended.

Williams had too much sense to underestimate Eliot's accomplishment, or even to undervalue it. But he felt as a betrayal and a defeat the effect of that accomplishment upon what I suppose we will have to call "the literary world." The passage I have just

The Poetry of William Carlos Williams of Rutherford

quoted is from *The Autobiography*. Unable to leave it alone, he returns to his complaint five brief chapters later:

> Then out of the blue *The Dial* brought out *The Waste Land* . . . I felt at once that it had set me back twenty years, and I'm sure it did. Critically Eliot returned us to the classroom just at the moment when I felt that we were on the point of an escape to matters much closer to the essence of a new art form itself—rooted in the locality which should give it fruit. I knew at once that in certain ways I was most defeated . . . I needed him: he might have become our advisor, even our hero. By his walking out on us we were stopped, for the moment, cold.[2]

I have made clear my own appreciation of the difficulty of Williams' predicament as a poet of Rutherford in his time, and also my respect for his perseverence and for what he accomplished. I can see why he saw *The Waste Land* as a setback. But the passages I have quoted are confusing, and they seem to come from confusion. The shifting back and forth between "I" and "we" is confusing. Who besides Williams was so resentful?

But just as confusing, and much more misleading, is the sense of betrayal and the idea that Eliot could just as well have stayed in the United States and become, like Williams, a poet of locality. All I am prepared to assume, because it is all that can be assumed fairly, is that these two poets chose their very different lives and ways because of needs that were imperative for each of them. They were personally nothing alike. They were different in character, in taste, and in social and cultural preferences. The idea that Eliot might have chosen to stay in America as an ally of Williams in the making of a distinctly American and local poetry is fantastical.

Strange as it may seem to those of us who came to literary consciousness in English departments still quaking from the publication of *The Waste Land*, that event is now eighty-eight years old, and the tremors have ceased. In the quiet that has followed I have thought often of my admiration and gratitude for the work of both poets. It has been a long time since I have wondered if there might be some inconsistency in this. If I am aware of the difficulties and obstructions that Williams found in his way, I am aware also of the personal anguish that so clearly informs Eliot's "impersonal" poems. In my own mind, at least, Williams' old quarrel with Eliot has lost its force. Their differences, to the considerable extent of my esteem for the work of both, are certainly of interest, but I am now moved also by their similarities.

&&

Eliot in his lifetime was a figure of international renown, stature, and authority, looming over the literary world from an elevation never attained by Williams. But neither of them was an infallible oracle. Each was limited by personal tastes and prejudices as you would expect any human to be. Eliot's professed allegiance to classicism, royalty, and Anglo-Catholicism has about the same supposable personal usefulness and general uselessness as Williams' espousal of the variable foot. As you would guess from their professed allegiances, Eliot's stance was cosmopolitan and aristocratic, Williams' democratic and local. You can imagine Williams as a royalist just about as readily as you can imagine Eliot delivering the ninth baby of an Italian peasant woman in New Jersey.

Eliot longed for impersonality. He was reticent, even aloof. He was a ventriloquist, most comfortable when speaking through masks, as Prufrock or Tiresias or Gerontian. Though we feel in his poems the authority of his own suffering of the disintegrations and estrangements of his time, his tone in his poetry as in his criticism is that of a person standing outside his subject. Williams, on the contrary, speaks characteristically as himself, and from within the place or presence that is his subject. And yet, paradoxically, Eliot seems a more likely ancestor than Williams of "confessional poetry." For Prufrock and others, Eliot invented a voice of self-revelation that is at the same time a voice of self-humiliation. Williams, even when he is speaking about himself, never claims the "courage" of revealing what most people would keep to themselves. In fact, though he speaks nearly always as and for himself, and often enough about himself, he observes a decent respect for his own privacy. He does not present himself, except in fun, as an odd or curious specimen. He does not offer himself as an object of contempt or sympathy.

Williams and Eliot

But to me, the most interesting difference between these poets is in their attitudes toward poetry itself.

Eliot's attitude seems by far to be the most common and conventional. He apparently abided by the principle that the purpose of poetry is to produce finely-wrought poems, highly "finished" artifacts worthy to be in the *Golden Treasury*. His standards of taste and workmanship, like his gifts, were rare and high. The relatively few poems he published have clearly met strenuous demands. You may find any or all of them disagreeable or unlikeable, but I don't think you can dismiss any of them as "a good try." This seems to be in keeping with his loftiness of demeanor, his personal reserve, and his stance or mask of critical distance. As he presents *The Waste Land* to us, it is a poem he has made, it has come from him, perhaps even from his experience, but it is finished, now separate from him, and he is standing outside it.

Williams was not a poet uninterested in excellence or in the "finished" poem. He was, as I have shown, passionately and unrelentingly interested in the technique, the art, of poetry. ("You cannot be / an artist / by mere ineptitude,"[3] as he knew, we may suppose, because he had tried it. He would not have minded our knowing that.) But because he was speaking inescapably from inside his subject, and his place, the purpose of his work, unlike Eliot's, was not immediately the finely realized art object, but rather a local product, the "no other speech than poetry" necessary "to reconcile / the people and the stones."[4] And so necessarily the focus of his interest is not on the indi-

The Poetry of William Carlos Williams of Rutherford

vidual poem, but on the continuum of his life's work, from ineptitude at the beginning to silence at the end. It was an unceasing process of trial and error, trial and failure, trial and success, which threw off a remarkable number of poems hard-earned and finely made, but which, as a process, never satisfied him or reached a point at which he could come to rest. It was by definition a circumstantial art—like that of Faulkner and Cézanne—an art that grows from local circumstances and also changes them at least by the addition of itself.

To use a metaphor I am unable to resist, Eliot in his work has the stance of a man showing a fine horse in a "halter class," in which the exhibitor, using a lead rein, presents the horse as a "finished" exemplar of its breed. Williams, by contrast, is always on the back of his horse, sometimes gracefully at one with it, sometimes not, but always at risk—which to the last he seems, young-mannishly, to enjoy.

≫

Before writing this book I spent many months reading the two volumes of *The Collected Poems of William Carlos Williams* and *Paterson*. Most of this work had long been familiar to me, but this reading was inclusive and fairly continuous. Every day before beginning my own stint of writing, I read a few poems or a few pages of Williams, until I had read every page, including most of the notes, of *The Collected Poems*. As I knew and realized again on this reading, the work ranges in quality

Williams and Eliot

from poems, especially in the early collections, that are slight or seemingly incomplete, tentative or awkward, to poems that are brilliantly achieved and completely satisfying. Of *Paterson* I have always had some doubts. I'm not convinced of the adequacy of the myth of "Mr. Paterson" ("A man like a city and a woman like a flower / —who are in love"⁵) which Williams seems to have difficulty keeping in mind. The many passages of prose quoted from books, newspapers, letters, etc., are invariably less interesting than the poetry, and, though maybe useful to the book's purpose or composition, they are not fully incorporated; some of them, on rereading, are simply dull. The structure seems less that of a single long poem than that of a collection of poems about a city. But *Paterson* is nonetheless an estimable book, containing some of Williams' best poetry. I have read it many times, always with pleasure.

My recent long reading, then, was unremittingly critical, for my debt to this poet is enduringly interesting to me, and I was trying to understand it. But the reading also was one of the most enjoyable of my life. I eagerly looked forward to it as a way of beginning my workday. And once I was past the earliest work, I was never disappointed, but was pleased to have my attention completely commanded and held by the poetry.

Years ago, after I started reading Williams, I thought he should have been more selective in publishing his poems; he should have published "only the best." By now I have pretty thoroughly changed my mind. I am sure of a considerable number of poems that I would call the best of Williams. But I don't think Williams' work exists for the sake of his or anybody's idea of his best poems. He was to the end of his life trying for something even better. In his struggle to make a poetry answerable to his need and suited to his place, he would try about anything, as we know because he published such a variety of things he tried. And so to whatever extent his poems are interesting in themselves, they are more interesting collectively as the record of his struggle. The nearly 1,200 pages of his poetry, taken as a whole, have a value and an interest, and they give a pleasure, that could not be suggested by any conceivable "selected poems."

∞

That two poets so different, personally and doctrinally, as Williams and Eliot could have been in significant ways concordant or alike is in itself moving. It is more moving in light of the probability that neither poet would have acknowledged any similarity at all.

But fundamental to the work of both men was the recognition that established verse forms could become exhausted. It is maybe not surprising but it is at least amusing to turn from Williams to Eliot's 1942 lecture, "The Music of Poetry," in which he reveals that his antipathy to the traditional scansion was probably as instinctive as Williams' own:

> I have never been able to retain the names of feet and metres, or to pay the proper respect to the accepted rules

of scansion . . . But certainly, when it came to applying rules of scansion to English verse . . . I wanted to know why one line was good and another bad; and this, scansion could not tell me.

Like Chaucer, Shakespeare, Wordsworth, and Williams, Eliot adhered to the "law of nature . . . that poetry must not stray too far from the ordinary everyday language which we use and hear." If he read it, Williams would have had to endorse the following:

> The music of poetry, then, must be a music latent in the common speech of its time. And that means also that it must be latent in the common speech of the poet's *place* [Eliot's emphasis].[6]

Both poets, moreover, recognized the modern world as a wasteland. Rutherford and Paterson provided as good evidence of this as London, and Williams saw it as clearly as Eliot. The seduced, forlorn typist of *The Waste Land* has her counterpart in Elsie of poem XVII of *Spring and All*. "Divorce," Williams wrote, "is / the sign of knowledge in our time . . ."[7] Eliot perhaps knew this better than Williams, but both poets knew it and attested to the pain of it.

Against the modern waste, both appealed to European traditions: Eliot, famously, to the classics and the integration of the Middle Ages; Williams, not so prominently, to the culture of the peasantry depicted by Peter Brueghel, the elder ("the suits of his peasants were of better stuff, hand woven, than we can boast"[8]). Thinking perhaps of Brueghel, whose work suggested to him the forsaken heritage of his immigrant patients, Williams wrote in the crucial poem XVII of *Spring and All* of

> young slatterns, bathed
> in filth
> from Monday to Saturday
>
> to be tricked out that night
> with gauds
> from imaginations which have no
>
> peasant traditions to give them
> character . . .[9]

For anybody willing to take it seriously, this poem, if Williams had written nothing else, would force a re-evaluation of American history.

Both Williams and Eliot also wrote of the Magi. Eliot typically used this subject once, definitively, in "The Journey of the Magi." Williams, in obedience clearly to a fascination, wrote four times, by my count, of the Nativity, including two poems about Brueghel's "Adoration of the Kings," one in *Paterson* V and another in *Pictures from Brueghel*. In both of the latter poems Williams, maybe in disrespect of the elegant and eloquent

Magus of Eliot's poem, suggests that the rich visitors were probably thieves.

And, what I think is most moving of all, both poets wrote late in their lives substantial works about love and forgiveness. Eliot's *The Elder Statesman* and Williams' "Asphodel, That Greeny Flower" both come from profound and painful knowledge, and each in its way seems an arrival hardly hoped for, "in hell's despite." [10]

Conclusion

. . . .

I don't think Williams' accusation against Eliot is valid. I don't think you can say specifically that Eliot's disinterest in Williams' project of an American poetry "rooted in . . . locality" retarded our poetical or cultural development. But though it led him, in this instance, to a regrettable extreme, Williams' project itself was valid. Our nation, from the standpoint of our country, was badly retarded in Williams' time, as he carefully knew, and it is worse retarded now. The most important reason for this is its failure to develop a culture, or rather cultures, rooted in locality. Because of racism, manifest destiny, geographic ignorance or wishfulness, equation of wealth with virtue and power with intelligence, and faith in universal technological "solutions," we have been blind to local differences or careless of them, or have held them in contempt. Our great centers of wealth and power—and, yes, of culture—live by the destruction of landscapes and communities that they consider "provincial," of which they know nothing, and for which they have taken no responsibility. Individual persons cannot justly be blamed for expatriating themselves or migrating to a great city. But a culture and an economy, which are nearly synonymous, are certainly blameable for ignoring and destroying their sources.

In fact, we have always needed distinctly local arts of poetry, storytelling, painting, and music in America, just as we have always needed distinctly local arts of agriculture, fishing, and forestry. Without such rootedness in locality, considerately adapted to local conditions, we get what we now have got: a country half destroyed, toxic, eroded, and in every way abused; a deluded people tricked out in gauds without traditions of any kind to give them character; a politics of expediency dictated by the wealthy; a disintegrating economy founded upon fantasy, fraud, and ecological ruin. Williams saw all of this, grieved over it, and accused rightly

> this featureless tribe that has the money now—staring
> into the atom, completely blind—without grace or pity,
> as if they were so many shellfish.[1]

There is not, in Eliot's work, any denial of the truth of this. I look upon his poems as a precious addition to the world and to my own life. I expect to be reading them with admiration and gratitude as long as I can read. But I am a writer whose home and subject is a small "provincial" community and landscape patently of the sort ignored or disdained by politicians, intellectuals, academicians, most scientists, and most writers, a place distracted by the technologies of communication and entertainment, its past mostly forgotten, its present obscured, its future for sale. Why, my friend Hayden Carruth asked me, to see if I could answer, has it been so important to a poet "on a farm in Kentucky to read the poems of a poet from the industrial mobocracy of northern New Jersey?"[2]

It has been so important because Williams' place was as marginal in its way as my own, and he devoted his life and art to it, not looking away or yearning toward some "better" place. Of all the writers known to me, Williams dealt most directly and explicitly with the complex cultural necessity of an ongoing, lively connection between imagination in the highest sense and the ground underfoot. Nobody had confronted more steadily the difficulties of such an effort in the face of the encroachments everywhere of industrial values, industrial exploitation, and the consequent loneliness of industrial individualism. For half a century his example has been always near to my thoughts, his poems always at hand. I have taken from them an encouragement and a consolation that I have needed and could not otherwise have found.

Conclusion

Notes

1. A Prologue

1. Robert Duncan, *Fictive Certainties* (New York: New Directions, 1985), 104.
2. William Carlos Williams, *The Collected Poems of William Carlos Williams,* vol. I, 1909–1939, ed. A. Walton Fitz and Christopher MacGowan (New York: New Directions, 1986), 4, 473. Hereafter *CPI.*

2. The Struggle Toward a Credible Language

1. William Carlos Williams, *Paterson* (New York: New Directions, 1963), 33–34.
2. William Carlos Williams, "A Negro Woman," *The Collected Poems of William Carlos Williams,* vol. II, 1939–1962, ed. Christopher MacGowan (New York: New Directions, 1988), 287. Hereafter *CPII.*
3. Ezra Pound, *ABC of Reading* (New York: New Directions, 1934), 14.
4. Williams, "To All Gentleness," *CPII,* 68–72.
5. Williams, "A Portrait of the Times," *CPII,* 9–10.
6. Williams, "Approach to a City," *CPII,* 108–109.

7. Williams, "The Gift," *CPII*, 430.

8. Williams, "El Hombre," *CPI*, 76.

9. Williams, "Young Woman at a Window," *CPI*, 373.

3. The Kind of Poet He Was

1. Williams, poem XVIII in *Spring and All, CPI*, 217.

2. Williams, "A Sort of Song," *CPII*, 55.

4. The Problems of a Local Commitment

1. Williams, *Paterson*, 30.

2. Williams, "Asphodel, That Greeny Flower," *CPII*, 323.

3. Ibid., 324.

4. Bruce Bawer, "The Poetic Legacy of William Carlos Williams," *The New Criterion* (September 1988): 15.

5. Williams, *Paterson*, 75.

6. Williams, "Tract," *CPI*, 72–74.

7. Williams, "The Problem," *CPII*, 239–240.

5. Local Adaptation

1. Stan Rowe, *Home Place* (Edmonton, Alberta: Newest Press, 2002), 42.

2. Stan Rowe, *Earth Alive* (Edmonton, Alberta: Newest Press, 2006), 34.

3. Ibid, 43.

4. Jean-Henri Fabre, "The Harmas," *The Life of the Fly* (New York: Dodd, Mead and Company, 1920), 13–14, 18.

5. Williams, *Paterson*, 33.

6. William Faulkner, *The Bear* in *Novels 1942–1954* (New York: The Library of America, 1994), 220–221.

7. William Carlos Williams, *The Selected Letters of William Carlos Williams*, ed. John C. Thirlwall (New York: McDowell and Obolensky, 1957), 278, 293.

8. Williams, "To the Ghost of Marjorie Kinnan Rawlings," *CPII*, 409–410.

9. Denise Levertov, *The Poet in the World* (New York: New Directions, 1973), 254.

10. Williams, "Portrait of a Woman in Bed," *CPI*, 88.

11. Ivan Illich, "The Wisdom of Leopold Kohr" (pamphlet published by the E. F. Schumacher Society, 1996), 14–15.

6. *"No Ideas But in Things"*

1. Williams, *Paterson*, 3.

2. Ibid., 11–12.

3. Williams, "To All Gentleness," *CPII*, 68–72.

4. Williams, "The Adoration of the Kings," *CPII*, 387–388.

5. Williams, *Paterson*, 263.

6. *Inferno*, XI, 109.

7. William Faulkner, *Intruder in the Dust*, in *Novels 1942–1954*, 368.

8. Ellen Davis, *Scripture, Culture, Agriculture* (New York: Cambridge University Press, 2009), 84.

9. Ibid., 152.

10. Ivan Illich, "The Wisdom of Leopold Kohr," 5, 6, 7.

11. Bernard Leach, "Integration," in *Every Man an Artist*, ed. Brian Keeble (Bloomington, Indiana: World Wisdom, 2005), 211, 212.

12. Edward Johnston, "Formal Penmanship Defined by the Thing," in *Every Man an Artist*, ed. Brian Keeble, 216.

13. Williams, *Paterson*, 265.

14. Michael Pollan, *In Defense of Food* (New York: Penguin, 2008).

15. Williams, "Asphodel, That Greeny Flower" *CPII*, 321–322.

16. Ibid., 324.

7. *A Matter of Necessity*

1. Williams, *Paterson*, 44.

Notes

2. John Lukacs, *Historical Consciousness* [7th printing] (New Brunswick, NJ: Transaction Publishers, 2009), 21.

3. Williams, "The Desert Music," *CPII*, 282.

8. *Two Mysteries: Inspiration and Talent*
1. Williams, "Asphodel, That Greeny Flower," *CPII*, 318.
2. Ibid., 325.
3. Philip Guston, quoted in *Guston in Time*, by Ross Feld (New York: Counterpoint, 2003), 37.
4. William Carlos Williams, *The Letters of Denise Levertov and Williams Carlos Williams*, ed. Christopher MacGowan (New York: New Directions, 1998), 8.
5. Williams, "The Sound of Waves," *CPII*, 115.
6. Denise Levertov, *The Poet in the World*, 265.
7. Williams, "Nantucket," *CPI*, 372.
8. Donald Davie, "A Demurral," *The New Republic*, April 20, 1987, 38.

9. *Art Conscious and Learnable*
1. Williams, "Asphodel, That Greeny Flower," *CPII*, 335.

10. *Line and Syntax*
1. William Carlos Williams, *In the American Grain* (New York: New Directions, 1925), 31–32.
2. Williams, "The Yachts," *CPI*, 388.
3. Williams, "The Cure," *CPII*, 67–68.

11. *The Three-Part Line*
1. Williams, *Paterson*, 78.
2. Williams, "The Artist," *CPII*, 267–268.
3. Williams, "Shadows," *CPII*, 309–310.

4. Ibid., 320.

5. Williams, "Paterson, Book V: The River of Heaven," *CPII*, 238–239.

6. William Carlos Williams, "Work in Progress," in *The Desert Music* (New York: Random House, 1954); and "Asphodel," *CPII*, 310–311.

12. Economy and Form

1. Williams, introduction to *The Wedge*, in *CPII*, 54.

2. Williams, "The Term," *CPI*, 451–452.

13. Measure

1. Williams, "The Desert Music," *CPII*, 275.

2. Williams, "Tribute to the Painters," *CPII*, 296.

3. Williams, *Selected Letters*, ed. John C. Thirlwall, New York: McDowell and Obolensky, 321.

4. Duke Ellington, song so titled.

5. Williams, *Selected Letters*, ed. McDowell and Obolensky, 325–326.

14. Rhythm

1. *Henry IV, Part II*, V.ii.4–5.

2. *Paradise Lost*, I.1–3.

3. William Carlos Williams, interviewed by Stanley Koehler, *The Paris Review* 32 (Fall 1964): 120, 127.

4. Martin Lings, *A Return to the Spirit* (Louisville, KY: Fons Vitae, 2005), 48.

15. The Structure of Sounds

1. Williams, "The Dance," *CPII*, 58–59.

2. Williams, poem XXII in *Spring and All*, in *CPI*, 224.

16. A Love Poem

1. Williams, "Coda" to "Asphodel, That Greeny Flower," *CPII*, 336.
2. Williams, "Writer's Prologue to a Play in Verse," *CPII*, 61.
3. Williams, "Asphodel, That Greeny Flower," *CPII*, 334.
4. Ibid., 335.
5. Williams, *Paterson*, 97.
6. Williams, "Coda" to "Asphodel, That Greeny Flower," *CPII*, 333–334, 336.
7. Williams, *Paterson*, 95.
8. Ibid., 78.
9. Ibid., 78.

17. More on the Context of Locality

1. Williams, *Selected Letters*, ed. John C. Thirlwall, New York: McDowell and Obolensky, 312.
2. Williams, poem XVII in *Spring and All* or "The pure products of America," *CPI*, 218.
3. Williams, *Paterson*, 30.
4. Williams, "Writer's Prologue to a Play in Verse," *CPII*, 59.
5. Czeslaw Milosz, *The Witness of Poetry* (Cambridge: Harvard University Press, 1983), 62–63.
6. Ibid., 107.
7. Robert Duncan, *Fictive Certainties*, 101.
8. Allen Tate, *Essays of Four Decades* (Wilmington, DE: ISI Books, 1999), 378.

18. The Prose of Spring and All

1. Williams, *Spring and All*, in *CPI*, 202.

19. The Eternal Moment and the Ground Underfoot

1. Williams, *Spring and All*, in *CPI*, 177–178.
2. Ibid., 185.

3. Williams, poem III in *Spring and All*, in *CPI*, 186.

4. Ibid., 187.

5. Williams, "The Cure," *CPII*, 67–68.

6. Williams, *Paterson*, 96–97.

7. Williams, "Shadows," *CPII*, 309–310.

8. Williams, *Paterson*, 95.

9. Williams, "Writer's Prologue to a Play in Verse," *CPII*, 61.

10. Hugh Kenner, *The Pound Era* (Berkeley: University of California Press, 1971), 387.

11. Williams, "Asphodel, That Greeny Flower," *CPII*, 318.

12. Williams, "To Daphne and Virginia," *CPII*, 246–247.

13. Williams, *Spring and All*, *CPI*, 189.

14. Williams, *Paterson*, 34.

20. Completeness

1. Williams, *Spring and All*, *CPI*, 193.

2. Ibid., 194.

3. Ibid., 194.

4. Ibid., 207.

21. Imagination, Invention, and Reality

1. Williams, *CPI*, 197.

2. Ibid., 198.

3. Ibid., 199.

4. Amanda Coomaraswamy, *Christian and Oriental Philosophy of Art* (New York: Dover, 1956), 19.

5. Samuel Taylor Coleridge, *Selected Poetry and Verse of Coleridge*, ed. Donald A. Stauffer (New York: Modern Library, 1951), 263.

6. William Blake, *A Descriptive Catalog*, in *Complete Writings*, ed. John Maynard Keynes (London: Oxford University Press, 1966), 576.

Notes

7. *Conversations with Cézanne*, ed. Michael Doran (Berkeley: University of California Press, 2001), 97.

8. Williams, *Spring and All, CPI*, 207.

9. Ibid.

10. Williams, *Paterson*, 65.

11. Williams, *Spring and All, CPI*, 219.

12. Williams, Introduction to *The Wedge, CPII*, 55.

13. Williams, *Spring and All, CPI*, 221.

14. Ibid., 225.

15. Williams, "Deep Religious Faith," *CPII*, 262–263.

22. *Williams and Eliot*

1. William Carlos Williams, *Autobiography* (New York: Random House, 1951), 146.

2. Ibid., 174.

3. Williams, "Tribute to the Painters," *CPII*, 296.

4. Williams, "A Sort of Song," *CPII*, 55.

5. Williams, *Paterson*, 15.

6. T. S. Eliot, *On Poetry and Poets* (New York: Noonday, 1961), 18, 21, 24.

7. Williams, *Paterson*, 28.

8. Ibid., 265.

9. Williams, poem XVII or "The pure products of America," in *Spring and All*, in *CPI*, 217.

10. Williams, "Asphodel, That Greeny Flower," *CPII*, 325.

23. *Conclusion*

1. Williams, *Paterson*, 265.

2. Hayden Carruth, personal letter, October 8, 2005.

Index of Poem Extracts

Index of Poem Extracts

Acknowledgments

Chapters 1 and 6 were first published in *The American Poetry Review*. Chapters 3 and 5 were first published in *The Sewanee Review*. I am grateful, of course, to the editors of both magazines.

For other help I am grateful to Tanya Berry, David Charlton, Don Wallis, Erik Reece, Robert Hass, Jack Shoemaker, Julie Wrinn, and Laura Mazer. All of these people have helped me more than they know, for I was moved to work harder on my manuscript just by the thought that they would read it.

Hayden Carruth—who, I am sad to say, will not read it, not in this world anyhow—corresponded with me at length about this project and gave me indispensable encouragement.

W.B.